—————— Last of The
Rare Book Game

THE GHOST.

Written by

Mr. Henry James, Mr. Robert Barr,
Mr. George Gissing, Mr. Rider Haggard,
Mr. Joseph Conrad, Mr. H. B. Marriott-
Watson, Mr. H. G. Wells, Mr. Edwin Pugh,
Mr. A. E. W. Mason and
Mr. Stephen Crane.

BREDE SCHOOL HOUSE,

December 28th, 1899.

7.45 P.M.

LAST OF
THE
RARE BOOK
GAME

George Sims

'And ever by some touch of keen
fragrance in the air, by some
mystery of added softness under
foot—ever a promise of something
to come, unguessed, delighting.'
—Kenneth Grahame

PHILADELPHIA
HOLMES PUBLISHING CO.
1990

Some of these articles have been printed in the Antiquarian Book Monthly Review, London Magazine *and the anthology* Inward Journey.

To Beryl

contents

During the ten year period in which I bought books, letters and manuscripts from Vyvyan Holland, Oscar Wilde's second son, the deals were so rich and varied that I would be hard put to it to choose the item of greatest interest. At that time many of Wilde's rarest books passed through my hands, together with letters and documents of considerable value. But if I had to select one book of great association appeal it would be Oscar Wilde's *Poems*, the copy inscribed by the author to his wife, Constance: 'To a poem from a poet.'

Some of the things V.H. sold to me had been given to him by various friends including Robert Ross, H.G. Wells, C.S. Millard and Charles Scott Moncrieff. Quite a number of books in his library had come from the collection of Edward Heron-Allen who had been a friend of Oscar Wilde and (reputedly) in love with Constance before becoming a friend of their son. Heron-Allen was a very unusual and versatile man of whom Sir Rupert Hart-Davis has given a good pen portrait in *The Arms of Time*, describing him as 'an amateur polymath of genius.' Under the pseudonym 'Christopher Blayre' Heron-Allen had published some bizarre works of fiction featuring bestiality, vampirism and demoniality. The only copies of his novels *The Purple Sapphire*, *The Cheetah-Girl* and *The Strange Papers of Dr. Blayre* which I have ever seen were those I bought from Vyvyan Holland.

In the afternoons I spent in Vyvyan's flat, 12 Grosvenor Court, Sloane Street, I learned a great deal by listening to him talk about books and authors. On one occasion he handed me a buff envelope which he had inscribed 'Bennett Notebook'; he said that it contained Arnold Bennett's first MS notes for the novel *Riceyman Steps*, and explained that he had been given it by Dorothy Cheston Bennett who was Bennett's second wife in effect if not in the eyes of the law (because Bennett's wife Marguerite would not divorce him). At that time I had not read *Riceyman Steps*, and did not fully appreciate the significance of the notebook, but I was keen to buy it nevertheless as I knew that Dr. John Gordan, Curator of the Berg Collection at the New York Public Library, was very interested in purchasing Bennett manuscript material. Dorothy Cheston Bennett's initials and address were on the inner front cover of the little book: there were some thirty pages of notes in pencil and ink, some being in shorthand. It was identified by an inscription in the author's hand, 'Notes for Riceyman Steps,' but it also had his earlier title, 'Resist Not Evil.' I was rather in the dark about the value of the notebook but I made an offer which Vyvyan accepted.

The following day I typed out a brief description and sent it off to John Gordan whom I considered to be one of my best customers. He promptly ordered it by telephone: I did not realize then that the Berg Collection already possessed the author's complete manuscript of the novel which had also been given to Dorothy Cheston Bennett, so that when John Gordan mounted an Exhibition of the New York Public Library, 'Arnold Bennett The Centenary of his Birth,' in 1967, the manuscript and notebook were shown together.

*   *   *   *   *   *   *   *   *   *

Enoch Arnold Bennett, the first of nine children, was born above a shop (run both as a draper's and a pawnshop by his father) at 90 Hope Street, Hanley in Staffordshire, on May 27, 1867. His father, also called Enoch, later used an inheritance to give up the shop and be articled to a solicitor; when his fortunes further improved he moved his family to a house at 205 Waterloo, Coburn, between Burslem and Hanley. Arnold Bennett's formal education began in 1877 when he entered the Burslem Endowed School, where he remained for five years. It was there that he first displayed some talent for writing: one of his earliest surviving manuscripts, that of the poem 'Courage', is dated one day before his fourteenth birthday. He subsequently entered the Middle School at Newcastle-under-Lyme but he stayed there only for a year, leaving in 1883 to enter his father's law firm.

While working for his father Arnold taught himself Pitman shorthand, and this skill enabled him to move to London in the winter of 1889 when he became employed as a shorthand clerk with a firm of solicitors, Le Brasseur and Oakley. Quite early during his stay in London he became friendly with an art teacher called Frederick Marriott and his wife; at their home he met artists like Edwin Rickards, musicians like Cedric and Herbert Sharpe, and a number of authors including George Sturt. In the spring of 1891 Bennett moved into 6 Victoria Grove to live with the Marriotts, and it was under their influence that he persevered with his writing and won a prize contest run by *Tit-Bits* for a parody of Grant Allen's melodramatic novel *What's Bred in the Bone*.

In 1893 Bennett wrote a serious piece of fiction, a short story called 'A Letter Home': it was pessimistic and realistic, showing the influence of the French authors he admired. It was refused by various popular magazines but was eventually published in Vol. VI of *The Yellow Book* in July 1895. Between the composition and appearance of this story Bennett took a decisive step in his career as an author by resigning his position with the solicitors and taking the post of assistant editor on a weekly publication, *Woman*, in January 1894. It was a part-time job for one full day and four half days a week, so it gave him more time for his own writing. While helping to edit *Woman* he used to review books under the name 'Barbara'; he also published some of his own stories as 'Strange Stories of the Occult by Sarah Volatile,' seven of which appeared in 1895. It was in the spring of the same year that he started his first novel which he called 'In The Shadow'; by the autumn he had written some 30,000 words and scrapped 25,000 of them. His second draft of the novel, titled *A Man from the North*, was completed in May 1896, six months before he was promoted to the editorship of *Woman*.

It was also in 1896 that Bennett began to write his *Journals*: this proved to be a mammoth work. Newman Flower, who edited the first edition of the first volume in 1932, commented: 'The fact that Arnold Bennett was able to compile *Journals* of over a million words, in addition to his large creative output, demonstrates the ceaseless impulse to write which was ever in him. What he thought, he had to write down. What he saw—the drama or the humour of a little episode in Life—he had to record, and usually in the form of a perfect pen-picture in miniature. It is fortunate that he did so, for these *Journals* reveal his personality more closely to his unknown admirers than all his novels . . . . '

John Lane accepted *A Man from the North* after a favourable report from his reader, John Buchan, but gave the author only a 5% royalty and took nearly two years to publish the book. On the title-page the author's name was given as E.A. Bennett, a form that was to be used for the next five years. Bennett wrote his second book, *Journalism for Women*, in eight weeks. John Lane rushed it into print after procrastinating over issuing the novel; Bennett was annoyed about this and took his revenge by demanding a 15% royalty instead of the 10% that Lane had offered. The book was published with a rather Beardsley-like cover design by Charles Robinson, a young artist whom Bennett described as 'Unkempt, pale, nervous . . . with a poor chin, and sensuous, tremulous eyes.'

In 1898 Bennett recorded in his journal his resolve 'To take up fiction for a livelihood . . . . To write popular fiction is offensive to me but it is far more agreeable than being tied daily to an office & editing a lady's paper.' But he waited until September 1900 before he resigned from *Woman*.

It was at the turn of the century that Bennett displayed his versatility as an author, when he wrote two musical plays; and his first published plays were brought out in November 1899, though the title-page of the book, *Polite Farces for the Drawing Room*, is dated 1900. For a short while then he lived at 9 Fulham Park Gardens before leaving London for a house in the country called Trinity Hall Farm in Hockliffe, Bedfordshire, in October 1900.

In September 1901 his first book of essays was published by Grant Richards. H.G. Wells, whom Bennett had met at the Marriott's house, pretended to be indignant at not being included in the book and sent him a letter on August 19, 1901, marked 'Private and Abusive,' referring to himself as 'an absolutely unique figure in contemporary literature . . . you are all wrong about the Fiction of the Popular Magazine on account of your failure to grasp ME.'

Bennett shared his farmhouse in Bedfordshire with his fatally ill father, mother and favourite sister Tertia. An early popular novel, *The Grand Babylon Hotel*, was serialized by Tillotson's before it was published in book form by Chatto & Windus who were to remain one of his principal publishers over the years. They also published his first novel to deal with life in the Potteries, *Anna of the Five Towns*; the book was dedicated 'with affection and admiration to Herbert Sharpe, an artist whose individuality and achievement have continually inspired me.' Over the next few years he wrote a number of plays and a great many articles which largely appeared in *T.P.'s Weekly*. He also wrote serious novels such as *Leonora*, potboilers including *Teresa of Watling Street*, together with *The Truth about an Author* and *How to Become an Author*.

The death of his father and a move to Paris seem to have had a liberating effect on Arnold Bennett's writing. The Parisian environment also stimulated him in other ways, enabling him to throw off old restraints and develop new habits and friends. At the beginning of 1905 he recorded a New Year's resolution in his journal: 'I firmly decided to marry.' The woman he chose was Eleanor Green, the daughter of an American business man then living in Paris; she was the sister of Julian Green who was to win fame as a novelist writing in French. Apparently she went along with Bennett's courtship without seriously considering marriage. He took various positive steps like leasing a new flat and buying furniture because there was a period of some weeks before Eleanor found the courage to say she could not marry him. On the 15th June 1906 Bennett recorded in his journal: 'At 5pm . . . in the forest of Fontainebleu I became engaged to marry Eleonora'; and on the 3rd August he wrote: 'At 11 am . . . my engagement to Eleonora was broken off . . . .' The traumatic effect of this was shown in that Bennett let his journal lapse for nearly a year. However, in 1907 he met an attractive French woman, Marie Marguerite Soulie, and married her on July 4th of that year.

The years 1905 to 1907 saw the production of several books by Bennett including *Tales of the Five Towns*, *The Loot of Cities*, *Sacred and Profane Love*, *Hugo*, *Whom God Hath Joined*, *The Sinews of War* and *Things That Interested Me*. Due to Bennett's journal it is known that the seminal scene which eventually led to his masterpiece took place on the night of November 17, 1903, when he went, as was his custom, to the Duval restaurant in the rue de Clichy and found sitting opposite to his usual seat 'a middle-aged woman inordinately stout in a simply awful light puce flannel dress.' This woman appeared to take an instant dislike to Bennett and twice moved her table before settling down to eat. Other patrons of the restaurant, and the waitresses, with whom she argued, were laughing at her; she was 'repulsive' and elicited no sympathy. 'But I thought,' Bennett wrote, recording the simple idea which he was to turn into a work of art, 'she had been young and slim once.' He had a vision of the tragedies that time and change and loneliness can bring about.

At first he thought of writing a short story, 'The History of Two Old Women,' giving the fat woman a sister: one sister was to live the most ordinary of existences, the other being 'a whore . . . living in guilty splendour.' Some five years passed before the draft of that short story was transformed into his great novel, *The Old Wives' Tale*. In September 1907 he finished the construction of the first part of it, and returned to writing about the two old women on October 8, having accumulated other material including the character of an unsympathetic husband, the terror of a French public execution by the guillotine, and the atmosphere of the siege of Paris. Bennett, who always took pride in being a professional author, kept to a strict regime while working on the book, leaving 'a clear three hours for it every morning.' It was a major work in every way including its length, some 200,000 words. He finished the book on the 30th August 1908, and Chapman & Hall published it on October 23 of that year.

books such as *How to Live on 24 Hours a Day* and *Literary Taste*, the plays *Cupid and Commonsense* and *What the Public Wants*, and the novels *The Glimpse*, *Helen with the High Hand* and *The Card* (a very popular, amusing book), before embarking on another 'serious' novel, *Clayhanger* (1910), the first of a trilogy, followed by *Hilda Lessways* (1911) and *These Twain* (1916). The last book was delayed by two events: a serious illness said to have been gastro-enteritis though it may have been typhoid fever, and the outbreak of war in 1914. The American publication of *These Twain* was a financial triumph for Bennett since he was paid $15,000 for the serialized version in *Munsey's Magazine*. Bennett kept a close eye on the financial rewards for his work, keeping a chart which recorded dates of publication, published prices and sales, etc. The chart shows that his most successful book was *The Card*, published in February 1911—between that date and December 31, 1915 it sold 53,330 copies.

During the 1914-1918 war Bennett wrote a number of articles for the *Daily News*, *New Statesman*, *Lloyd's Weekly Newspaper*, *Illustrated London News* and the *Saturday Evening Post*. It was in this period that his marriage became progressively more unsatisfactory, so that in addition to his country house Comarques at Thorpe-le-Soken in Essex he rented separate establishments in London for his wife and himself. His first biographer Dudley Ward wrote: ' . . . Marguerite was growing more and more unhappy. The one thing she wanted was constant and demonstrative affection, and she received increasing neglect.'

Throughout 1919 and 1920 Bennett spent more and more time by himself in a maisonette at 12B George Street, Hanover Square. It was another prolific period for novels and journalism, and he wrote four plays in quick succession. He was stimulated to start one play called *The Bright Island* when he learnt that *Sacred and Profane Love* had taken over 16,000 dollars during its first week in New York.

Bennett's failing marriage finally broke down in 1921 after Marguerite went on a recitation tour in France and Italy, a part of which she spent in the company of a man called Pierre Legros. The couple agreed to separate and Bennett made his wife a generous settlement, giving her £2,000 a year providing that sum should prove to be not more than a quarter of his net income, £5,000 capital at his death, and an income for life of two-thirds of his estate after the £5,000 had been paid.

A scene that Bennett wrote about in his journal in 1913 remained in his mind when he began to work on *Riceyman Steps*. On the 30th January 1913, on the day after he attended the first English production of

1913, on the day after he attended the first English production of *Rosenkavalier*, he noted: 'Courting. Tonight sheets of rain, strong wind. I put on over-shoes and mackintosh to go to the corner of the street to post. Several times lately about 10 p.m. I have noticed a couple that stand under a big tree at the corner next to the pillar-box, shielded by the tree-trunk from the lamplight. They stand motionless, with hands nearly meeting round each other's backs, tightly clasped. They were there tonight. The man was holding an umbrella over them. Can't see what sort of people they are. In the first place I don't like to intrude and in the second place the shade is so dark.'

The main inspiration for *Riceyman Steps* came from a visit that Bennett made to a bookshop in Southampton in the summer of 1921. Bennett knew a good deal about second-hand bookselling, having dabbled in it as a young man and being a life-long bibliophile; the characters of the couple who ran the Southampton shop made a big impression on him and he first thought of writing a short story about two misers in a shop, jotting down notes in the little book he inscribed 'Resist Not Evil.'

In the following year the novel took shape as he began to fall in love with Dorothy Cheston, an architect's daughter whom he met when she took part in a Liverpool production of one of his plays, *Body and Soul*. This was in February 1922. Dorothy Cheston first came to his flat in George Street on the day of the Boat Race that April, but they did not meet regularly until the autumn.

Dudley Barker commented on *Riceyman Steps*: 'He created the novel out of almost no material. A few visits to Clerkenwell gave him a whole new constricted fictional world as real and touchable and smellable as he ever made from the five towns. Elsie and Joe he got from a chance observation, one rainy evening, of two lovers standing still on a street, in an embrace under an umbrella.'

Margaret Drabble, in her Bennett biography, ably summarized the plot: ' . . . Mr. Earlforward has an antiquarian book shop and he is a miser. He has a charwoman called Elsie, who has a shell-shocked lover called Joe. Earlforward marries, near the beginning of the novel, a neat, economical-seeming little widow, Mrs. Arb, who has moved into a neighbouring shop. They celebrate their wedding by visiting Madame Tussaud's, a visit which recalls the visit to the Louvre which the wedding party makes in Zola's *L'Assommoir*, yet more proof that Bennett was returning back to his first exemplars. The conflict in Earlforward between miserliness, ill-health, and a genuine wish to do the right thing by his bride is very finely done. They live together, and she is increasingly horrified by his increasing meanness. They both fall ill, are nursed by the devoted Elsie, and both, in grim circumstances, die. That is all there is to it. What makes it so remarkable is its accuracy, its compassion, its feeling for the quality of working-class life and morality, its physical detail . . . . The setting is drab, the characters are neurotic rather than tragic, and yet the novel isn't depressing. There is something wonderful about it. How amazing, how various and odd, one says to oneself on finishing it . . . .'

The novel was completed on the 17th March 1923 and the author was convinced that it was good; he wrote to André Gide that it was 'rather better than some of my novels,' but his close friend Harriet Cohen said that he was quite excited about the book. On publication its quality was immediately recognized by both critics and readers, and it was awarded the Tait Black Novel Prize, the only literary prize he ever received.

George Moore's reaction to *Riceyman Steps* was recorded in Bennett's journal for 'Monday, 31 March 1924—I met George Moore last night at the Phoenix performance. He said he wanted me to go and dine with him and that he would tell me about *Riceyman Steps*—a lot of things that I don't know (he said). Then he told me. He said it was the only really objective novel ever written, and very original. (I knew from others that he thought very highly of it.) He said, "It has no form whatever, *no* form. It is not very carefully written—it is adequately written. It has no romantic quality. Yet it holds you. A bookseller crosses the road to get married—that's all. It is disturbing to think that hundreds (he should have said millions) lead their lives just like that. The book is FACT (he emphasized the word several times) and that's all . . . ." '

I shall leave the last words on *Riceyman Steps* to the author himself, written in September 1919 when he was hard at work on *Imperial Palace*: 'And when I have finished it and corrected the manuscript and corrected the typescript and corrected the slip-proofs and corrected the page-proofs, and it is published, half the assessors and appraisers in Britain and America will say: "Why doesn't he give us another *Old Wives' Tale*?" I have written between seventy and eighty books. But also I have only written four: *The Old Wives' Tale*, *The Card*, *Clayhanger* and *Riceyman Steps*. All the others are made a reproach to me because they are neither *The Old Wives' Tale*, nor *The Card*, nor *Clayhanger*, nor *Riceyman Steps*. And *Riceyman Steps* would have been made a reproach too, if the servant Elsie had not happened to be a very "sympathetic" character. Elsie saved *Riceyman Steps* from being called sordid and morbid and all sorts of bad adjectives. As if the "niceness" of a character had anything to do with the quality of the novel in which it appears! But authors are never satisfied.'

2.   — GRANT RICHARDS: PUBLISHER

Franklin Thomas Grant Richards was born in Glasgow on October 21, 1872, when his father was Assistant Professor in the Latin Department at the University of Glasgow. He spent his infancy in Lyme Regis, Dorset, living with his mother's parents, and his childhood in Oxford where his family lived at No. 7 Beaumont Street. His first school was Langdale House and then he went to the City of London School at which time he stayed in lodgings with a schoolmaster near the Crystal Palace.

A diary he kept in 1887 shows that bookdealing of a kind began when he was fourteen:

> May 5. I have sold Johnstone 2 books for 4/6. They are boys books which I do not now want. He has not yet paid me.

> May 10. I am no longer French Monitor as I was kicked out for being out of my place. I have sold Brooks 3 books for 6/3. I got on better in extra Chemistry today as my things were in order.

The diary also listed books he then owned:

> ' . . . Sheridan's Plays the first book I bought with my own money, De Quincey's *Confessions of an Opium Eater* that I had also bought myself, *Treasure Island* and Frank Stockton's *Rudder Grange*. *Treasure Island* had been given to me as a Christmas present in 1886 by Herbert Richards; some other kindly person had given me at the same festival *King Solomon's Mines*. In a week or so one of those vexatious people who are always pulling a child up by the roots to see how he is growing asked me which I liked best. In my then literary surroundings I created some scandal by voting unreservedly for Rider Haggard. Some of my elders tried by argument to make me change my opinion.

R.L.S. was a great man in the eyes of the Grant Allen household and a friend of the family, whereas Rider Haggard was a novice at the art of story-telling. My uncle protested at such coercion. "Leave him alone, Emily; let the boy like what he likes," he said to my mother.'

Grant Richards was always on good terms with his uncle Grant Allen, and later on was to publish his books, but his business career started with Hamilton, Adams & Co. who were wholesale booksellers. Through Grant Allen, again a benign influence, an interview was arranged with Arthur Miles who was the head of the firm: 'Anyhow he engaged me: I was to start work on September 1st, 1888, at 8.45 in the morning at 32 Paternoster Row; I should be paid at the rate of twenty pounds a year; and he hoped that I should prove worthy of the recommendation on the strength of which he had given me a hearing. Twenty pounds a year! Eight shillings a week! One shilling and fourpence for each of the working days of the week! Great!'

When he began the bookselling job Richards took lodgings at 62 Sutherland Avenue, husbanded his money and managed to spend some evenings each week at the theatre at a time when Henry Irving and Ellen Terry were to be seen at the Lyceum. He did a two year stint of bookselling before being offered the position of assistant to W.T. Stead who was editing the *Review of Reviews*. He went to live in the Hampden Residential Club in Euston and to work in a large flat in Mowbray House, Norfolk Street which had a splendid view over the Thames. Among the various things he had to do was the compilation of a kind of guide to the flood of books published at Christmas: 'For most of the hours of the day I thought of nothing but books, their writers, and their publishers, and I suppose I had as much knowledge of the outward appearance of what was being published as anyone not commercially connected with the trade.' It was at this time that he met the publishers John Lane and Elkin Mathews, and some of the authors who were to be published by The Bodley Head.

Over the next few years G.R. moved more and more in literary circles and he left the residential club in Euston to take a flat at 10 Barton Street in Westminster. 'At number 10 Barton Street I was happier than I had ever been, Frederick Whelen joined me after a while, taking the lower floor, and to my rooms came a succession of men who found this Westminster backwater so unexpected and congenial that they followed my example and discovered rooms for themselves . . . .'

A love affair with France, more or less life-long, began with his first visit to Paris in the spring of 1892. Richards crammed a lot into his week there, walking the streets, finding good, cheap restaurants, braving the Rat

Mort and meeting William Rothenstein who then lived at 23 rue Fontaine: '. . . my host had even more character than his environment. Small, yes; you saw it the first time: you did not notice it again. Small and put together with unusual neatness, and, yes, dressed with unusual neatness too. Spectacles. Black hair. Very small feet. An effect rather Japanese.' They shared a simple lunch and their friendship began. 'There was a salad made as salads were never made in the England I knew, and the cauliflower was cooked as they must cook cauliflower in heaven . . . . I felt there was no place in the world like Paris, that to be a young man and a painter in Paris was to be the most favoured of God's creatures, that to be the friend of a painter in Paris was the next best thing . . . .'

It was in 1892 that G.R. moved from Westminster to the Rossetti Garden Mansions in Chelsea and met a number of other authors such as H.G. Wells, Richard Le Gallienne and Frank Harris: 'But to go back to Frank Harris. He would talk his party silly, but no one of them but would agree that his was magnificent talk. And when he wasn't talking he was telling stories, the magnificent stories that he afterwards published . . . . Grant Allen told me that Harris was very coy when it was suggested to him . . . . "But your stories are in the very front rank, Harris," his listeners would say to him. "Yes—you think so. But are they equal to Maupassant's best?" '

During the next few years, while still working for Stead, Richards was meeting more authors and making other contacts in the world of printing and publishing. His own career as a publisher began, appropriately enough for a man who always conducted his affairs with style and élan, with a party: 'It was in Henrietta Street at midnight, Dec. 31, 1896, that the passer-by might have heard, and been surprised at hearing, the strains of music, the noise of a hired piano to be exact, and of young voices raised in song, proceeding from Number 9, a house whose facade certainly did not suggest that it could in any way be dedicated to revelry. The passer-by no doubt wondered . . . . I have often wondered myself. How could I have brought myself to greet the momentous New Year in my brand-new office with a party? . . . I should have been darting nervously about the premises with a duster, measuring racks and shelves and hanging up pictures, generally preparing for the arrival of my staff at nine o'clock and tuning my soul against that eventful moment when, figuratively, we should take down the shutters and the business of Grant Richards: Publisher would be open to the world . . . .'

Grant Richards was able to start his publishing business at the age of twenty-four because his father was willing to lend him five hundred pounds while Grant Allen and another uncle contributed nine hundred pounds between them: 'So fourteen hundred pounds was the capital on which I could rely; it was not a great deal of money, but to my sanguine mind it was enough to begin with . . .. Grant Allen was sanguine: he had the liveliest belief in my nose for a good book or a coming author (had I not introduced him to the work of H.G. Wells and Richard Le Gallienne?) . . .. Even the wise Edward Clodd, secretary to the London Joint Stock Bank as well as a writer of repute, thought my venture might succeed . . ..'

And, indeed, Edward Clodd, rationalist and good friend of Thomas Hardy, was the author of the first book to be published by G.R. The title was *Pioneers of Evolution from Thales to Huxley*: 'I had wanted him to write a history of the evolutionary movement but he preferred the more piecemeal way of attacking the subject. I bought the copyright for the odd sum of one hundred and seventy-one pounds, sixteen shillings and sixpence . . ..'

Richards' next deal was to arrange that his uncle Grant Allen should write a series of Historical Guides, the first one being on Paris. When that was accomplished he approached Bernard Shaw with the suggestion of publishing his plays: 'I told him that my dearest wish was to be his publisher, to produce his plays, to produce all his books, to be publisher in ordinary and publisher extraordinary to Bernard Shaw . . ..'

Shaw replied to this enthusiasm with caution:

29 Fitzroy Square, W.
8th November, 1896

Dear Sir,

As far as I have been able to ascertain—and I found my opinion on what I have been told by Heinemann, Lane and Walter Scott of their experience with dramatic works by Pinero, Wilde, George Moore, etc.—the public does not read plays, or at least, did not a very few years ago. Have you any reason to suppose that it has changed its habits? . . .

Shaw continued to argue in the same pessimistic vein when he met Richards for a walk in London, late one evening after a theatrical first night: ' . . . that I was crazy to think of printing his plays, that to do so would ruin me in no time, that there was no sufficient public for them yet, and so on and so on. It seemed to me more than doubtful whether he was even attempting to hear what I had to say . . ..' But G.R. was not to be deterred by all this caution and dubiety; he had the enthusiasm of youth which an older person often finds infectious: 'In theory at least George Bernard Shaw

13

had agreed that I should produce the Plays. The fact that J.T. Grein as Henry and Co. had already produced *Widowers' Houses* without attracting many buyers, counted for very little in my mind, did not in any way reduce the elasticity of my steps as I walked home . . . . Having the promise of Bernard Shaw on my first list of announcements, I had indeed made sure that I should succeed in putting myself on the map.'

At the same time Richards was developing other possibilities, capitalizing on his ideas which are a young person's most important asset. Two early moves of his were to persuade E.V. Lucas to compile an anthology for children, and to commission a novel, *One Man's View* by Leonard Merrick. Another of Richards' notions, which was to prove a failure, was the launching of an annual, *Politics in 1896*, with his cousin Frederick Whelen as editor and G.B. Shaw as one of the contributors, tackling a favourite subject, Socialism. ' . . . The thing was a ghastly frost. I lost two hundred and fifty pounds on it . . . .'

While he was putting these editorial ideas to the test, Richards was also busy finding out as much as possible about printing and other aspects of book production. That he succeeded in his determination to make books with his imprint physically attractive will be apparent to anyone who has handled them. In 1927 Gerard T. Meynell of the Westminster Press wrote to the T.L.S. about its 'Printing Supplement': 'You mention those who have done something to make their books look better, but as far as I am able to see you do not mention Grant Richards, who was one of the first publishers to produce decent-looking books.' Among the printers with whom G.R. commissioned books were T. and A. Constable, R. and R. Clark, and C.T. Jacobi at the Chiswick Press who printed his attractive edition of Walter Leaf's *Versions from Hafiz*.

There were some nine books in Richards' first list, printed at the end of Edward Clodd's book: a volume of reminiscences by Sir Hugh Clifford, the Grant Allen book on evolution, a novel by Leonard Merrick, *Real Ghost Stories* edited by W.T. Stead, the E.V. Lucas anthology, etc. Late in his life G.R. looked back on those early days in Henrietta Street with considerable nostalgia: ' . . . they were the only months during which as a publisher I enjoyed any protracted peace of mind. To repeat myself: I *was* a publisher; I had an office; I was being kindly spoken of in other papers than the *Mail*; the books I produced were having their fair share of notices; the literary world of London was aware of my existence; authors were bringing me their manuscripts to consider; I was able to commission books; I could summon young painters to see me and ask them to execute this and that piece of work; I could rejoice in seeing Bernard Shaw on one day and E.V. Lucas or Richard Le Gallienne on another . . . .'

Another aspect of the business which Richards researched in those early days was the craft of paper-making. He was fortunate enough to contact Harold Bayley of the firm of Spalding and Hodge who carried on their business in an old warehouse in Drury Lane, within a stone's throw of Henrietta Street: 'Realizing Bayley's qualities, I put myself in his hands . . . . In Arthur Waugh's book of publishing reminiscences there is a tribute to Harold Bayley. He deserves it. In a drawer of my desk I have now a folder of papers cut to various sizes. He made and gave it to me in the spring of 1897. Throughout the whole of my publishing life I have relied on his advice.'

In his own room at the Henrietta Street offices Richards had a trap-door which gave immediately into a stone-paved cellar, 'A Sweeny Todd trap-door,' and on occasion the behaviour of some authors made him think of fitting it with a lever that could be operated from his desk: 'The real trouble is when the visitor won't get up and go and, although he has nothing to say, will insist on saying it again and again at inordinate length. I have glanced at my clock a dozen times and yet have had no real effect on him. It is his day out and he is going to make the most of it . . . . Much too often, if he has already achieved the dignity of being an author of a book published elsewhere, he spends the first quarter of an hour of his visit in explaining why he cannot possibly continue publishing his books with the publisher which published his last. The firm is old-fashioned, or it doesn't advertise, or its reader had the impertinence to suggest an alteration or an omission. He must tell you all about it, and not seldom does he reflect, without shadow of reason, on the solvency and honesty of the house which has spent time and money on him.'

It was E.V. Lucas who suggested that G.R. should publish a novel by Richard Whiteing, then a middle-aged journalist. The book was called *No. 5 John Street*; published in 1899, it was a considerable commercial success and after its success other publishers flocked round the author. He described to Richards one such interview:

' "We should very much like to bring out your next novel, Mr. Whiteing. I hope you will be free to bring it to us."

"That's odd, Mr. ------. You had the chance of publishing *No. 5 John Street* and you refused it without apparent hesitation."

Mr. ------ smiled: "We all make mistakes. That was my damned reader. I can't read everything myself. If I did I should never have allowed your book to go back to you . . . . How many have you sold?"

"I don't know: I haven't had a statement yet. Ten thousand—fifteen—I can't say."

"Well, it doesn't matter. We should have sold twice—thrice—as many. We should have advertised it more; we should have pushed it more. . ."''

Another young publisher, R. Brimley Johnson, who had set up in business at much the same time as Grant Richards, brought him Chesterton's first book: ' . . . he hadn't much self-confidence and when it was open to him to publish a book of serious verse by a young friend, Gilbert Keith Chesterton, he brought the manuscript to me rather than run any kind of risk on his own account. The book was *The Wild Knight*. Brimley Johnson liked it and why he did not whip up his courage was always an enigma to me, for he did publish the humorous *Greybeards at Play* later on . . . .'

Readers of Grant Richards' entertaining book about his publishing career, *Author Hunting* (1934), will search in vain for any reference to Frederick Rolfe ('Baron Corvo'); probably the experience of publishing the paranoid 'Baron' and suffering several nips from his crab-like claws made Richards prefer to forget him. But their relationship is skillfully delineated in A.J.A. Symons' *The Quest for Corvo*. In Chapter Eight, 'The Strange Historian,' Symons tells of their meeting in 1899 and how ' "Frederick Baron Corvo" was engaged to produce a history of the rise and fall of the Borgia family which should be at once a gallimaufry of living pictures and a studious chronicle . . . . For payment he was to receive a sovereign a week (for not more than seven months), ten pounds on publication, and twenty-five pounds on the issue of a second edition. In return he sold, irrevocably, all rights. Not very generous terms; but they were his own suggestion, and the best he was to get during the whole of his life . . . .'

In a letter that is not dated but was written in November or December 1899, 'Baron Corvo' made an early report to Richards on their agreement:

Hogarth Club
Bond St., W.

Dear Mr. Richards,

I have got through the first week on 18s.10d., which I think is a bit of a triumph! It was achieved by the simple expedient of cutting dinner: and it has left me furious for work. Now I find the evenings intolerable after the B.M. closes; and think you might let me have something to read by way of change. Mss. for choice, *for which I shall not expect you to pay unless you like*. It's *reading* I want *hic et nunc*.

V ty, Corvo

In February 1900 'the Baron' wrote from Jesus College, Oxford to report again: 'The Borgia book is progressing. I should very much like to have photographs of the various portraits etc., which I selected some weeks ago; for, with these before me to assist the human air, I shall be able to work without let or hindrance, as long as my health endures the strain. I must say that I find living on a pound a week, while working as intensely as I do, to be a very difficult task. May I suggest the desirability of increasing that amount to thirty shillings—a sum which would save me many petty worries? Of course, I do not for a moment propose any interference with the agreement which I have made with you; but that the extra ten shillings should come out of the sum which you are to pay me on publication . . . .' Richards did not reply to this letter. Symons commented: 'This pathetic, modest request went unanswered. Perhaps the young publisher with a business to establish would or could not go beyond his contract. Shortage of money was not, however, Corvo's only trouble. His artistic conscience was alarmed by reductions proposed in the number of illustrations planned for the book; he fought for portraits and medallions like a wild-cat for its young . . . .'

The letters from 'Corvo' to Richards changed tone several times; they became 'by turns querulous, vindictive and threatening.' And when the manuscript of his Borgia book was submitted to an 'expert' reader, Rolfe/Corvo 'exploded like a bomb: "Dear Mr. Grant Richards" became at once "Dear Sir", and Rolfe's letters took on an instantaneous tone of sullen dignity . . . .' By April 1901 'Corvo' was writing: 'Dear Sir, I cannot regard your letter as being in any way a straight reply to mine; and you leave me no option but to take professional advice.'

In 1952 I decided to publish the letters from Frederick Baron Corvo to Grant Richards under the imprint of the Peacocks Press. I asked Guido Morris to print an edition of 200 copies at The Latin Press in Cornwall; he printed them on Hodgkinson hand-made paper and had them bound in Hodgkinson hand-made paper boards; he produced an attractive little book. I dedicated the book to the memory of Grant Richards and used, as an epigraph, a quotation from the *Chronicles of the House of Borgia*: 'No man, save One, since Adam, has been wholly good. Not one has been wholly bad. The truth about the Borgia, no doubt, lies between the two extremes.' I thought by doing this to underline to the reader that in publishing only one side of the correspondence I was giving only one side of the argument, but no doubt I was being over-subtle. A reviewer in the T.L.S. took me to task over this and said that the book should have had a preface to explain the situation. A prompt response to this review was a letter I received from a member of the Richards family threatening me with legal action for libel on G.R. I took the letter to a solicitor who gave me a dusty answer and the advice to 'wait and see.' Fortunately I was also able to show the letter to Martin Secker who had been a good friend of Grant Richards over a long period. Martin offered to write on my behalf to the Richards family, and I heard no more about the 'libel.' However I did issue a leaflet which could be inserted in the book:

BARON CORVO
LETTERS TO GRANT RICHARDS

Postscript

In fairness to the memory of Grant Richards (an imaginative and courageous publisher) it should be understood that many of the grievances vented by Baron Corvo in these letters are imaginary. The letter dated 11 March 1902 is the last of the series relating to CHRONICLES OF THE HOUSE OF BORGIA but the author's sense of grievance did not last long enough to prevent him from proposing a fresh alliance and more publications to Grant Richards a few years later.

The Peacocks Press

By the turn of the century Grant Richards was married and had moved to 19 St. Loo Mansions in Flood Street, Chelsea. He had also established a friendly relationship with G.B. Shaw and was much involved in producing books to satisfy the great man who was apt to write letters like this:

Dear G.R.

I return a couple more sheets—all I've got—for press. If you look at pp. 17, 25, 26 & 27 you will see that I have made a faint protest against the whiteness of some of the lines. You might suggest to them that they need not justify to avoid dividing a word at the end—that it is better to divide a word than have a loose line making a streak of whitey grey through the black. Caxton would have printed your name Gr-ant Richa-rds at the end of a line sooner than spoil his page with rivers of white.

The great thing is to get the colour even. Besides, since we are substituting spaced letters for italic in underlined words, it is important that the spacing should be regular and rather narrow, so as to make the spacing distinctive . . ..

Another of Richards' important author relationships was that with A.E. Housman. Grant Richards wrote of him at some length in *Author Hunting* and was later to devote a book to him called *Housman 1897-1936*. 'Now when I commenced publisher *A Shropshire Lad* was perhaps of all the books the one I most wanted for my list. Kegan Paul having published it, not at his own but at the author's expense—the fact was generally known in literary and publishing circles—there was little to prevent another publisher approaching Mr. Housman in the hope of securing it for his own list . . . .' Richards wrote proposing himself to be the publisher for a second edition of the book and received a polite letter from Housman to the effect that the book was still available from Kegan Paul, but a year or so later the poet called in at the Henrietta Street offices to say that the first edition had been exhausted and Richards might have the book. Housman did not wish to receive any payment for it and suggested that if a profit was made then part of it should go towards reducing the price of future editions. Richards tried to give an impression of Housman at their first meeting: ' . . . Precise. Yes, precise perhaps, in the way that a scholar may be precise, precise in speech, bearing, clothes. But not precise in any uncomfortable way. Certainly his spirit showed no sign of effervescence and he did not use ten words where five would do; and perhaps his aspect was, until I had seen his smile, a little sombre.'

From Chelsea G.R. moved to 51 Great Marlborough Street, just off Regent Street, and in the heart of London's West End. He also acquired a country house at Cookham Dene where guests including Housman were entertained at weekends. Richards' first wife was Italian but in his books of reminiscences he devotes only a few lines to the marriage: ' . . . so I will confine myself to saying that my wife bore me children and that the union was dissolved.'

Nevertheless his wife was to give her name, or her initial, to the re-birth of the business after G.R. encountered financial difficulties. In *Housman . . .* Richards dealt with this upset succinctly: 'Towards the end of 1904 difficulties beset me, difficulties which I was not to overcome. I, who had never been possessed of much capital, but had perhaps been tempted beyond prudence by too much credit, had been overtrading and spending too much money. I took, I had to take, what came to me in punishment, and I am not prepared to say that I did not deserve it . . . . But all was not lost. I was to receive much kindness . . . .'

Among those who reacted with kindness was Housman who wrote him friendly letters, although the bankruptcy meant problems for a projected edition of Housman's *Juvenal*. Richards wrote: 'Yes, the Juvenal was practically ready for publication. Who was to publish it? My affairs were in the hands of the Court; I was for a time debarred from starting another business. What could be done? With the assistance of my creditors the difficulty was surmounted. A new business was started of which I was to be, and did immediately become, manager. "I am proud to be your first author," Housman wrote to the proprietor on June 1, 1905. His encouragement, his approval, meant everything; and in due course the firm of E. Grant Richards opened an office at 7 Carlton Street, Regent Street.'

Richards' enterprise in writing to authors paid off when he contacted John Masefield and arranged to publish *Salt Water Ballads* which was issued in November, 1902. Five hundred copies were printed and G.R. subsequently disposed of the story, still current among some dealers, that many copies of it were lost in a fire at the warehouse of the binders, Leighton, Son and Hodge. He went on to publish several more books by Masefield, ' . . . but in the end I lacked courage—which in a publisher is often synonymous with capital . . . . To my shame, in 1909 I developed cold feet. I was offered *The Tragedy of Pompey the Great*. I dilly-dallied with it until the author had no further patience and asked me to send the manuscript back to him . . . . To tell the truth, I had allowed my ledgers to influence me. It was a folly. No publisher worthy of his job, if he has any money left in his banking account, will, if he can help it, allow an author whose work he respects and admires to go elsewhere. In the long run things will come right—and even if they don't—well, he will have the happiness and satisfaction of having been true to his own taste . . . .'

Richards' perceptiveness also prompted him to write to John Galsworthy after reading his masterpiece, *The Man of Property*; the letter did not immediately bring him Galsworthy as an author, but they did get to know each other and occasionally dined together. At one dinner G.R. suggested to Masefield and Galsworthy the launching of a new quarterly, to be called 'The Peacock', but nothing came of the project. Later on Galsworthy offered Richards his book *A Commentary*: 'No doubt he was influenced by the fact that after a reverse I was building up a fresh list. It was not one of his best books but it was characteristic. A book of sketches rather than of short stories, it was full of the sense of pity that informs all his work.'

It is puzzling that James Joyce is nowhere mentioned in *Author Hunting*, yet there are more than a score of references to Grant Richards, as the publisher of *Dubliners* and *Exiles*, in Richard Ellmann's biography of Joyce.

In September 1904 James Joyce, acting on Arthur Symons' suggestion, sent the manuscript of his poems *Chamber Music* to G.R., and he quoted part of Richards' reply in a letter to his brother, Stanislaus, from Pola, Austria on February 7, 1905. Somehow the publisher managed to lose this MS and asked for another copy, only to turn it down because Joyce could not help pay for its production.

On October 15, 1905 Joyce wrote to Richards about another project, his book of short stories about Dublin: 'I do not think that any writer has yet presented Dublin to the world. It has been a capital of Europe for thousands of years, it is supposed to be the second city of the British Empire and it is nearly three times as big as Venice. Moreover, on account of many circumstances which I cannot detail here, the expression Dubliner seems to me to bear meaning and I doubt whether the same can be said for such words as "Londoner" and "Parisian", both of which have been used by writers as titles.'

Joyce's manuscript of *Dubliners* was sent to Richards on December 3, 1905. The publisher liked it, as did his reader, Filson Young, and he accepted it for publication on February 17, 1906, signing a contract in the March of that year. Affably, G.R. enquired about the author's circumstances and Joyce replied with a letter from Trieste, hinting at frustration and impatience: 'I am an English teacher here in a Berlitz school. I have been here for sixteen months during which time I have achieved the delicate task of living and supporting two other trusting souls on a salary of £80 a year . . . . My prospects are the chance of getting money enough from my book or books to enable me to resume my interrupted life . . . .'

Joyce also sent Richards an additional story, 'Two Gallants', for the book and it led to catastrophe when the publisher sent it off to his printer who marked passages and objected to it before going on to raise points about the other stories. In a letter dated May 5, 1906 Joyce asked what the printer objected to: 'Is it the small gold coin in the former story or the code of honour which the two gallants live by which shocks him? His idea of gallantry has grown up in him (probably) during the reading of the novels of the elder Dumas . . . . His marking of the first passage makes me think there is priestly blood in him: the scent for immoral allusions is certainly very keen here . . . .'

Correspondence about these matters continued with a stiffening of position on both sides. On June 23, 1906 Joyce wrote defensively: 'It is not my fault that the odour of ashpits and old weeds and offal hangs round my stories. I seriously believe that you will retard the course of civilization in Ireland by preventing the Irish people from having one good look at themselves in my nicely polished looking-glass.' However all his letters were to no avail, and the 1906 edition was abandoned, the only surviving fragments of it today being two proof pages from 'Two Gallants' preserved in the Houghton Library at Harvard University.

After several bitter years of frustration and disappointment about his writings the climate changed a little for Joyce towards the end of 1913. He had written despairingly to Richards who replied, in a letter dated November 25, desiring to see the MS of *Dubliners* again. Good news reached Joyce in January 1914 because Richards agreed to publish though he stipulated that the author would not receive royalties on the sale of the first 500 copies. Proofs of the 1914 edition reached the author in April, and he returned them quickly with press notices of *Chamber Music* to be used in the advertisements. An edition of 1250 copies of the book was published on June 15, 1914 and it received reasonably good reviews. A few critics found the stories cynical or pointless, but the book gained Ezra Pound's praise in *The Egoist*, and Gerald Gould thought it pointed to the emergence of a writer of genius. By May 1, 1915, 379 copies of the book had been sold but this figure included the 120 copies which Joyce had been compelled to buy. When Joyce complained that this was disastrous Richards blamed the poor sales on the war.

Three years later, under the terms of his contract with Richards, Joyce submitted the MS of his play *Exiles*. Joyce's agent J.B. Pinker remonstrated with him about this contract and the author replied with an exasperated letter: 'You have written to me several times of what you call the "disastrous" and "dreadful" character of my contract with Mr. Richards and ask why I signed it. I signed it in 1915 after a struggle of 9 years for the publication of my book—written in 1905 . . . .. The type of the abortive first English edition (1906) was broken up. The second edition (Dublin, 1910) was burnt entire almost in my presence. The third edition (London, 1914) is the text as I wrote it and as I obliged my publisher to publish it after 9 years. Possibly the terms of *his* contract are unfair. I neither know nor care anything about that matter—so long as he does with the help of his printer the work he undertakes to do for me . . . .' The contract for *Exiles* was dated August 31, 1917 and is now preserved in the Yale University Library. The play was published on May 25, 1918, but the author's pleasure in this occurrence was diminished by the trouble he was having with iritis in both eyes, the operation for glaucoma the previous year not having been a complete success.

An approach by Grant Richards that paid off was to Thomas Burke whose short stories, *Limehouse Nights*, G.R. published in 1916. Today the stories seem only mildly risqué and it is hard to credit that at the time it was thought that the publication might arouse 'the authorities'. ' . . . things looked for a while as if trouble was pending. Arnold Bennett told Burke that the possibility of securing a conviction was seriously discussed at headquarters, and that he himself feared the worst.' In the event *Limehouse*

Nights escaped the censor and was a success, to be followed by the same author's novel, *Twinkletoes*. D.W. Griffiths offered five hundred pounds for the film rights of the book of short stories and eventually agreed to one thousand pounds, producing the silent classic, *Broken Blossoms*, starring Lillian Gish and Donald Crisp.

A book which did create a great stir on publication was Alec Waugh's novel about life in a public school, *The Loom of Youth*, written when the author was only eighteen. The book came to Richards from S.P.B. Mais who had taught the boy at Sherborne, and it was issued with a preface by Thomas Seccombe, then a professor at the Royal Military College at Camberley where Alec Waugh was posted, prior to his being gazetted to the Machine Gun Corps. The reviews that the book received guaranteed its success. A typical one was in the *Nation* of September 15, 1917: 'I have read few books that have interested me more than Mr. Waugh's *Loom of Youth*. It is in one respect an almost miraculous production. Here is a boy of eighteen who diaries his school life, reproduces its talk and atmosphere, and builds up a merciless memorial of its evils and short-comings . . . . It seems to me that it is a revolutionary work—if only the parents of England will read it, and having read, act on it . . . .'

In 1912 Grant Richards began another career, as a novelist, when he wrote *Caviare*. This was to be followed by seven more novels, *Valentine* (1913), *Bittersweet* (1915), *Double Life* (1920), *Every Wife* (1924), *Fair Exchange* (1927), *The Hasty Marriage* (1928) and *Vain Pursuit* (1931). In June 1912 Housman saw a notice about *Caviare* and on July 2 he wrote: ' . . . I see you are coming out as a novelist. "Huitres" or "Crevettes roses" or some such title.' Housman went to Italy at the end of that summer and sent a letter on September 7 from the Hotel de l'Europe, in Venice, to acknowledge a copy of the book which G.R. had sent him: ' . . . I read with great interest all through, though the Monte Carlo parts perhaps are not equal to the Parisian and American. These last seem to me particularly good. I have just seen a favorable review in the Telegraph. I hope you will not now take to writing poetry or editing Manilius . . . .'

Another of the authors whom Richards published, 'Ernest Bramah' (Ernest B. Smith), also wrote to congratulate the publisher turned author: ' . . . I got your book the other day and without saying in the language of the facile reviewer that I found it literally impossible to tear myself away until the last page was reached, I certainly found it too easy to neglect other things once I had got into it. At first, I confess, the epicureanship of your amiable Charles put me off a little ("I shall have the steak-and-kidney pudding" fits me) but—if criticism is not an impertinence—I found the page become better and better, and the last half of the book—all the American portion and the end—is quite irresistible . . . .'

In 1915 Grant Richards was married for the second time, to 'a Hungarian lady, younger by eighteen years than myself,' but again, in his published books, he is very reticent about her and other matters concerning his personal life. We do know that, early in the same year, G.R. and Housman made a joint trip to the Riviera. It seems odd to think that such journeys were possible while the Great War was being waged in northern France. ' . . . There was, we supposed, some danger of the ship being mined or torpedoed, but I recall that Housman neither expressed or showed any nervousness on that score. He went to our cabin, exchanged his hat for the small and very out-of-date cricket cap that he so often wore, stretched himself out and, before we had left the harbour he was, or appeared to be, asleep . . . . I found Housman a delightful companion, equable in temper, seldom moody, a good talker, appreciative of attention, polite to those who smoothed his path. And untiring . . . . And best of all, from my point of view, he told me, as we travelled up to London on our return, that he had enjoyed every day of the holiday, and that he had never known a more agreeable and able courier.' Years later Richards was to deal with the Riviera at some length in his travel book, *The Coast of Pleasure* (1928).

In the spring of 1900 Richards had published the first book by 'Saki' (H.H. Munro), *The Rise of the Russian Empire*; in 1915 he issued the second book, *Vainglory*, of an even more exotic author, Ronald Firbank. Martin Secker had declined to publish *Vainglory* but suggested that G.R. was a possibility. Richards read the manuscript during the 1914 Christmas holiday, and at a meeting with Firbank on December 28 of that year explained the financial arrangements under which he would bring out the book: these included a payment of £80 by Firbank to cover the costs of production and another £20 for advertising, 'especially in the "Morning Post".'

Ronald Firbank had the reputation of being the butterfly of the book world, but he could be very much down to earth when he thought that was necessary. He took a considerable interest in the production of the book, supplying a Felicien Rops crayon drawing to be reproduced as the frontispiece and on the dust-wrapper; he paid £12.17.6d. for this and urged that the artist be named on the d.w., fearing the drawing, the upper part of a colored sketch showing a nude in a black hat, might be mistaken for a Beardsley. Firbank also wanted lettering with 'smartness & style'; he said he would be 'willingly Viennese just for once.' And he supplied samples of paper for the dust-wrapper to Mr. Wiggins who dealt with book production at Grant Richards Ltd. 'He found very smooth paper unpleasant, but thought "light rather coarse Venetian paper would be just the thing".' He urged Richards to have the edges of the book stained green; green, he wrote, would be 'a quite thrilling contrast' to the black covers. Finally he sent instructions about the printing; the printers 'were not to replace any of those Capitals—they would not know where to put them & the result would be like almonds in a trifle.' Subsequently he wrote to the publisher, on 31st March 1915 when he had seen an early copy of the book: 'A line to tell you how delighted I am with *Vainglory*. In such charming looks who could have the heart to be horrid?'

Over the next eleven years Richards published all but one of Firbank's novels: *Inclinations* (1916), *Odette* (1916), *Caprice* (1917), *Valmouth* (1919), *The Princess Zoubaroff* (1920), *Santal* (1921), *The Flower Beneath the Foot* (1923) and *Concerning The Eccentricities of Cardinal Pirelli* (1926). The author financed the last book, as he always did, but its publication was still delayed by the publisher's mounting financial difficulties. Brentano's, the author's American publishers, decided against publication of the book on 'religious and moral grounds,' fearing that the 'outspokenness of the book regarding the life of the Cardinal and particularly church matters' would alienate readers. Firbank wrote to Carl Van Vechten from Cairo on 17 December 1925: 'The Cardinal is being held up by Richards, who is I hear being made a bankrupt. Fortunately I am producing the book in England myself, so that its debut may be looked for directly G.R. can snatch a calm hour from the Bailiffs.' Despite the author's optimism various factors, including the General Strike, combined to delay the book, and when it was finally issued Firbank had been dead for some six weeks.

Continuing financial problems and bankruptcy hampered Grant Richards' publishing career a good deal in the late 1920s, but he managed to issue some books including two by Llewelyn Powys, *Black Laughter* and *Thirteen Worthies*; he also published John Cowper Powys's novel *Ducdame*. As his publishing activities declined G.R. turned more to writing. After *The Coast of Pleasure* and two novels, he wrote the autobiographical *Memories of a Misspent Youth 1872-1896* which was published by Heinemann in 1932. This had as a frontispiece a pastel portrait of the author, drawn by William Rothenstein in Paris in 1893. It also had an Introduction by Max Beerbohm: ' . . . I ask myself, "What is the peculiar quality of the pleasure that these Memories have been giving me?" One of the elements of this pleasure, no doubt, is that so many of the things that impressed the young Grant were impressing me in just the same way. I was his elder by only two months. We must have begun to "take note" almost simultaneously. We were neck-and-neck Victorians. He tells us that at Christmas in 1886 somebody gave him *Treasure Island*, and somebody else gave him *King Solomon's Mines*. I received those very gifts at that very moment; and I cordially shared my little coeval's opinions of their rival merits . . . as is well known by all who have read his novels, Grant Richards (albeit a publisher) is a born writer, a man who knows just what he wants to say, and can say it—say it always lightly, firmly, vividly, amusingly, endearingly . . . .'

In 1934 Hamish Hamilton published Grant Richards' *Author Hunting*. On July 16 of that year Max Beerbohm wrote from Rapallo to send back the galley proofs of the book, assuring him that it was as good as *Memories* . . . .: 'As vivid and amusing and well-observed and characteristic . . . . I don't think (as you do) that the bulging-out of the G.B.S., in proportion to the rest, matters at all. After all, he is the most remarkable of living writers. And the fact that he is neither an artist, in any sense of the word, nor a human being in *very* many senses of the word, doesn't detract much from his immense value to the world. And one of his great good points, his genuine kindness and helpfulness, comes out strong in your account of him and his many—his not too many—but rather too dreadfully technical and trady—letters.' As an epigraph to the book, Richards printed part of a letter that Shaw had written him on May 23, 1934: '. . . You should call your book The Tragedy of a Publisher who Allowed Himself to Fall in Love with Literature. The publisher who does that, like the picture dealer who likes pictures or the school-mistress who gets fond of her pupils, is foredoomed. A certain connoisseurship in the public taste is indispensable; but the slightest uncommercial bias in choosing between, say Bridges' "The Testament of Beauty" and a telephone directory, is fatal . . . .'

Grant Richards' career as an author came to an end with the publication of his book *Housman* by the Oxford University Press in 1941. This is of considerable interest for the information it gives regarding the poet from the days of the second edition of *A Shropshire Lad*, published by G.R. on September 14, 1898, up to a Housman letter dated January 20, 1936—the last that Richards received. In this letter, written some three months before his death, Housman commented: 'I was 3 weeks in the Nursing Home unable to answer letters. I am now back here and lecturing but with no strength for anything beyond my actual work . . . .' The book is also of importance in that it contains ten appendices by various authors on different aspects of Housman, including 'Personal Recollections' by Percy Withers,

'Dates of Housman's Poems' by Sir Sydney Cockerell, 'The Manilius Dedication . . . ' by Edmund Wilson, 'Housman considered mainly as a Scholar' by Professor O.L. Richmond, etc.

Martin Secker's friendship with Grant Richards started when Martin inherited a sum which he thought would help to establish him in a publishing career: 'When I was in my early twenties I came into a legacy of £1,000 . . . .' He then wrote to three publishers, William Heinemann, John Lane and Grant Richards, suggesting that he would be willing to invest this amount in return for a salaried position. In his article, 'Publisher's Progress', in *The Cornhill*, Summer 1973, Martin gave an account of their various reactions. William Heinemann declined the offer: 'He pointed out kindly that the amount of capital I proposed to invest was too small to interest him, and in a fatherly fashion he pointed out the dangers I should incur in venturing into so hazardous a trade. Mr. Richards likewise "could not see his way" although he was distinctly interested in the proposal and hoped that something might be arranged at a future date if I were still of the same mind. Our interview took place in Carlton Street, off Lower Regent Street, whither he had moved, after a financial reconstruction, from spacious premises on the west side of Leicester Square. Now he occupied a small Georgian corner house with steep stairs and tiny rooms. That first meeting with Grant Richards remains very clear in my mind, not only for the charm and friendliness of his manner, but by reason of the fact that a few years later, after I was in business on my own account, he was to become my greatest friend in the publishing trade.'

In 1935 Grant Richards, who had known more financial ups and downs than most publishers, wrote to Martin Secker who was being threatened with a bankruptcy petition by Walter Hutchinson in respect of an £800 debt to a printer controlled by Hutchinson:

4 Cranley Place, SW7
12 vii 1935

Nothing, my dear Martin, is ever quite as bad as it threatens to be and, even if Hutchinson is in no way to be deflected, I cannot relinquish my conviction that there is some way out. I, who have suffered, as you know, more than most people through reverses of fate, have always found some compensations. The great thing is not to allow oneself to be hustled into some unwise step. I should sit tight now, if I were you, till Hutchinson makes some move . . . . And through the whole of Saturday and Sunday think of everything else rather than your

difficulties. I shall be here early on Monday (8 Regent Street). After all
you have a brave history behind you.

G.R.

Their friendship continued until Richards' death, and after that Martin
was to preserve the memory of it by using the imprint 'The Richards Press
Ltd.' When Martin reprinted *Author Hunting* in 1960, Alec Waugh
contributed an Introduction which is as lively as it is perceptive: 'I first met
Grant Richards in the spring of 1917 when I was nearly nineteen and he
was in his middle forties. He had just accepted my first novel and I called
on him in his offices, across the way from Ciro's. I knew more or less what
to expect. My father knew him well. "Grant Richards," he said, "is the
best-dressed publisher in London and he wears an eyeglass." He was certainly
an impressive person. He was the first "man of the world" that I had met,
and today, forty years later, I have not met anyone who fits that role more
effectively. He looked and behaved as the young Arnold Bennett from the
Potteries dreamed of looking and behaving. He was supremely knowledgeable
about food and wine and clothes and travel, about the practical ordering of
existence . . . . The preceding paragraphs may have given the impression
that Grant was managing and "bossy" but that was not the case. It was a
sense of assurance, of self-confidence, that he diffused. He was never in a
hurry, he was never flustered, his voice was warm, his manner suave. His
bearing suggested that the present was agreeable, and that no matter what
the past had been the future would be better still. His monocle heightened
this atmosphere of well-being. It was not attached to a cord; it had no frame;
it stayed in place. Only a very composed man can wear a monocle . . . .
He wanted more out of life than publishing could give him; a trait that Shaw,
temperamentally, could not understand, because he had not the clue to it
inside himself; but Dreiser understood it, very well. To him Richards was a
character out of Balzac, a middle-aged Rubempré. "Towards gambling, show,
romance, a delicious scene, he carries a special mood. Life is only significant
because of these things. His great struggle is to avoid the dingy and the dull
and escape if possible the penalties of encroaching age . . . . Just one hour
of beauty is his private cry. One more day of delight, let the future take care
of itself . . . . He had a delicious vivacity which acted on me like wine."
With that kind of nature he inevitably took more out of the business than
it could afford . . . .'

Grant Richards died in January 1948 at Monte Carlo, after a trying
illness during which he was looked after by his wife Madeleine (to whom
he had dedicated his book *Housman*: 'To my wife who shared with me Alfred

28

Housman's friendship'). An obituary appeared in *The Times* written by E.S.P. Haynes; as a valediction it contained a slightly bitter paragraph: 'So, too, his real instinct for friendship, his unruffled amiability, his handsome attire and monocle concealed a recurrent lack of scruple which startled many of his best friends in literary and other circles, and would have permanently alienated them but for his genius in conciliation and cajolery.'

No doubt some of Richards' traits were upsetting to his friends but in considering his achievements it seems more appropriate to end with a quotation from Alec Waugh, based on long experience: ' . . . Reading *Author Hunting* in 1934 one felt one was following the story of a failure. But now, a quarter of a century later, ten years after Grant's own death, one feels one is reading the story of a success. Events have fallen into focus. We can see the literary history of an era in perspective. We can see how much Grant achieved . . . . There are those who set their names as publishers on books which are part of our eternal heritage; men who enrich the world by the work they do in it. Who can think of the eighteen-nineties without remembering Elkin Mathews, John Lane and Leonard Smithers? Who could write of the years 1910 to 1925 without paying tribute to Martin Secker? And the name of Grant Richards will always be honored on account of the authors he sponsored.'

Once upon a time, but not all that long ago, it was possible for book-dealers to make discoveries, and occasionally to secure great bargains, at the London auction rooms. All dealers whose experience goes back beyond the 1970s will remember the period when books and manuscripts were coming on the market in profusion and at a rate which did not allow the auctioneer's staff to examine each lot with the close scrutiny that now obtains. Most dealers therefore have their tales of bargains which often came about by serendipity. In a wine carton of Swinburne pamphlets I bought the extremely rare first issue of Swinburne's first book, *The Queen Mother and Rosamond*, 1860 (T.J. Wise believed that only the poet's proofs and personal copies had the Pickering title-page). And a true example of serendipity occurred when I bought a portfolio of Aubrey Beardsley magazines and ephemera without having looked at it, only to find that it contained a few original drawings by A.B.

My purchase of *Guy Domville* in 1966 was not really a case of serendipity nor a great bargain but it came very close to it. In the summer of that year I received a catalogue from Hodgson's book auction rooms in Chancery Lane. One lot caught my eye as it described a small collection of Henry James books, including a play. For some strange reason, which I cannot explain, I thought that the play might be *Guy Domville* of which only a few prompt copies were privately printed for the cast in 1894. I went to London and examined the James lot. The books generally were of no interest to a first edition dealer, but when I opened a small volume bound in half-green calf I found the title-page to be what I had suspected:

GUY DOMVILLE
Play in Three Acts

Printed—as Manuscript—*for Private Circulation only.*
London: Printed for J. Miles & Co., 195, Wardour Street, Oxford
Street, W. 1894.

*   *   *   *   *   *   *   *   *   *

In one of Henry James' notebooks, in his 'summing up' of 1881, he spoke of working for the theatre as 'the most cherished of all my projects,' and of 'the dramatic form' as 'the most beautiful thing possible,' but not till some ten years later did he settle to that project in earnest. The stage came to dominate his life between 1890 and 1895 and it did so, in the first place, because the actor Edward Compton (husband of the American actress Virginia Bateman and father of Compton Mackenzie) wrote to him suggesting that he should dramatize *The American.* James did this and the play opened in Southport, Lancashire, on 3rd January 1891, being greeted with enthusiasm by the first audience. For the play James created a happy ending with the hero being finally able to marry the charming young widow, Claire de Cintré. Many critics wrote unfavourably about the play which they thought spoilt the novel by adding elements of farce and melodrama. Edward Compton, in a long overcoat with outsize buttons, played a caricature of an American. The reviewers were also critical of the young American actress, Elizabeth Robins, who played Claire de Cintré. Despite a largely unfavourable press Compton took the play, after touring, to London, staging it at the Opéra Comique Theatre.

In London too *The American* had mixed reviews: 'Mr. James has given us a play which is more than sufficiently descriptive, and far from vigorously dramatic.' Despite an attendance by the Prince of Wales, which brought a flurry of publicity, the play only ran for seventy-six performances and James made little money out of it.

The first hint of *Guy Domville* is in the author's notebook covering the autumn of 1892:

Situation of that once-upon-a-time member of an old Venetian family (I forget which), who had become a monk, and who was taken almost forcibly out of his convent and brought back into the world in order to keep the family extant. He was the last *rejeton*—it was absolutely *necessary* for him to marry. Adapt this somehow or other for today.

In the event James did not adapt the idea to his 'today' but set the play in the eighteenth century: in the first act a young English Catholic is on the point of taking holy orders when he inherits a fortune and is persuaded that he must assume its responsibilities. The second act shows him disillusioned with worldly society, and in the third he reverts to his original decision.

The year 1894 was a fruitful period for James, for he wrote two fine stories 'The Death of the Lion' and 'The Coxon Fund' which appeared the next year in his book *Terminations*; he also made a visit to Venice to help sort out the papers of his friend Constance Woolson who had committed suicide close to the Venetian palazzo which she rented. Returning from Venice, he became much involved in the plans of the popular actor-manager George Alexander to produce *Guy Domville* at the St. James's Theatre. During December 1894, while the play was in rehearsal, James was saddened by the news of the death of his friend Robert Louis Stevenson at the age of forty-four ('this ghastly extinction of the beloved R.L.S.'). The cast for the play was a distinguished one: Alexander played Guy Domville and was supported by H.V. Esmond, Marion Terry, Evelyn Millard and Irene Vanbrugh. W.G. Elliot played Lord Devenish. Elliot recorded some advice from James about his part: 'Well do I remember a good score off me at rehearsal by the author—who was too charming and kindly a man ever to have made it knowingly—when he came up to me and said in his curious, always fishing for the absolutely correct word, way: "Elliot, in your playing of this riotous—I mean 'dissolute'—old—I should say 'middle-aged'—peer, may I suggest—'hint' would be the better word—to you that you should endeavor—'try'—to make him as much of a gentleman as is feasible—'possible'—to you!"'

Guy Domville opened at the St. James's Theatre on the evening of Saturday 5th January, 1895. Edmund Gosse wrote: 'George Alexander was sanguine of success, and to do Henry James honour such a galaxy of artistic, literary and scientific celebrity gathered in the stalls of the St. James's Theatre as perhaps were never seen in a London playhouse before or since. Henry James was positively storm-ridden with emotion before the fatal night, and full of fantastic plans. I recall that one was that he should hide in the bar of a little public-house down an alley close to the theatre, whither I should slip forth at the end of the second act and report "how it was going".'

On January 3, 1895 James wrote a letter to Gosse: '*Don't* after all, trouble to come to seek me on the Saturday evening at the little nestling pub; for I have changed my policy. I recognize that the only way for me to arrive at 10 o'clock with any patience is to *do* something active or at least positive; so I have had the luminous idea of going to see some other play. I shall go and sit at the Garrick or the Haymarket till about 10.45—or 11—and then I will come to the theatre; at which moment you will be, I trust, in your enraptured stall. All thanks for the charitable intention I frustrate. The 2nd act isn't over till 10.15, or 10.30 even, and it is to get *to* that period (at the pub. or at home) that would be the devil.'

James later wrote to his brother William about the first night: 'On the night of the 5th, too nervous to do anything else, I had the ingenious thought of going to some other theatre and seeing some other play as a means of being coerced into quietness from 8 to 10.45. I went accordingly to the Haymarket, to a new piece by Oscar Wilde . . . *An Ideal Husband.* I sat through it and saw it played with every appearance (so far as the crowded house was an appearance) of complete success, and *that* gave me the most fearful apprehension. The thing seemed to me so helpless, so crude, so bad, so clumsy, feeble and vulgar, that as I walked away across St. James's Square to learn my own fate, the prosperity of what I had seen seemed to me to constitute a dreadful presumption of the shipwreck of *G.D.*, and I stopped in the middle of the Square, paralyzed by the terror of this probability—afraid to go on and learn more.'

'F. Anstey' (T.A. Guthrie) recorded a description of the First Night, Act I: 'I was one of the audience at the first night of his *Guy Domville* at the St. James's—a very terrible first night indeed. It was a costume play; the period early Georgian; George Alexander played the name-part and was extremely well supported, while the stage sets designed by Edwin Abbey were charming. For a time all seemed to be going well, the dialogue, being Henry James's, was exquisitely phrased, and the house listened to it attentively. But before the first act was over it was clear that the play was not gripping the audience; the coughs which are infallibly a sign of it grew more and more frequent. However, the house was full of his friends and admirers, and the applause at the end of the act was loud enough, though it came chiefly from the stalls and the dress circle.'

The artist W. Graham Robertson described the worsening effect of Act II: 'With the next act came a change. The author had done a dangerous thing in dropping most of the first-act characters and introducing a new set in whom little interest was taken. The excellence of the opening was now a drawback, the audience wanted more of it; they longed to follow the fortunes of Marion Terry and sulkily refused to be interested in the doings of Miss Millard. An elderly actress (Mrs. Edward Saker) entered in a costume which struck them as grotesque. As a fact the dress was a particularly fine one, but it wanted wearing; the huge hoop and great black hat perched upon a little frilled under-cap should have been carried by one filled with the pride of them and the consciousness of their beauty. But at the unexpected laughter the actress took fright, she became timid, apologetic, she tried to efface herself. Now the spectacle of a stately dame whose balloon-like skirts half filled the stage and whose plumes smote the heavens trying to efface herself was genuinely ludicrous, and the laugh became a roar. After this the audience got out of hand; they grew silly and cruel and ready to jeer at anything.' He added, about the disastrous Act III: 'the last act, with its lovely White Parlour and the longed-for return of Marion Terry, almost pulled things together again, but by this time the hero's continual vacillations between his lady-loves struck the demoralized house as comic, and when he changed his mind for the last time the irreverent let themselves go.'

H. G. Wells was also there on the first night, acting as critic for the *Pall Mall*. In his reminiscences he wrote: 'Alexander at the close had an incredibly awkward exit. He had to stand at the door in the middle of the stage, say slowly, "Be keynd to her . . . *Be* keynd to her" and depart. By nature Alexander had a long face, but at that moment, with audible defeat before him, he seemed to have the longest and dismallest face, all face, that I have ever seen. The slowly closing door reduced him to a strip, to a line, of perpendicular doom. The uproar burst like a thunder-storm as the door closed and the stalls responded with feeble applause . . . .'

The rowdy crowd in the gallery had become increasingly vocal with one or two wits making telling points. When Alexander, in the last act, delivered the line, 'I'm the *last*, my lord, of the Domvilles,' someone shouted, 'It's a damned good thing you are!'

H. G. Wells commented upon the author's appearance on the stage: 'Disaster was too much for Alexander that night. A spasm of hate for the writer of those fatal lines must surely have seized him. With incredible cruelty he led the doomed James, still not understanding clearly how things were with him, to the middle of the stage, and there the pit and gallery had him. James bowed; he knew it was the proper thing to bow. Perhaps he selected a few words to say, but if so they went unsaid. I have never heard any sound more devastating than the crescendo of booing that ensued. The gentle applause of the stalls was altogether overwhelmed. For a moment or so James faced the storm, his round face white, his mouth opening and shutting, and then Alexander, I hope in a contrite mood, snatched him back into the wings.'

Leading critics, including Clement Scott and William Archer, reviewed the play favourably and G. B. Shaw gave it a particularly friendly notice in the *Saturday Review*, but it only lasted a month, being taken off on 5th

February 1895 ('whisked away to make room for the triumphant Oscar') and replaced by *The Importance of Being Earnest*, which Alexander had hurried into production.

That the author was not completely downcast is shown by an entry in his notebook, made on Saturday 12th January, 1895: 'Note here the ghost-story told me at Addington (evening of Thursday 10th), by the Archbishop of Canterbury: the mere vague, undetailed, faint sketch of it—being all he had been told (very badly and imperfectly), by a lady who had no art of relation, and no clearness: the story of the young children (indefinite number and age) left to the care of servants in an old country-house, through the death, presumably, of parents. The servants, wicked and depraved, corrupt and deprave the children: the children are bad, full of evil, to a degree. The servants *die* (the story vague about the way of it) and their apparitions, figures, return to haunt the house and children . . . .' This tale was, of course, transformed by the Master's art into *The Turn of the Screw*.

Again proving that he was not crushed by the play's failure, nor complaining about the waste of so much time and energy, James wrote to W. D. Howells: 'I mean to do far better work than ever I have done before. I have, potentially, improved immensely and am bursting with ideas and subjects—though the act of composition is with me more and more slow, painful and difficult.' And the next day, January 23, 1895, he made a confident entry in his notebook at home at 34 De Vere Gardens, London W.8: 'I take up my *own* old pen again—the pen of all my old unforgettable efforts and sacred struggles. To myself—today—I need say no more. Large and full and high the future still opens. It is now that I may do the work of my life. And I will . . . .'

* * * * * * * * * *

When I attended that summer sale at Hodgson's I had made up my mind to bid up to £400 for the James lot but was not at all optimistic of securing it at that price; I imagined that several first edition dealers might have discovered that the collection included what is possibly Henry James's rarest book. So I was prepared for the bidding to be brisk and to quickly pass my limit: it turned out quite otherwise. When the lot number was reached there was a pause so I made an opening bid of £5; another pause, and for a few moments I envisaged a very great bargain indeed. Then my bid was raised across the room by someone I could not see. I increased the bid to £10 and again it was raised. This time I half stood up and saw that the other bidder was 'Dusty' Miller, who ran the firm of Frank Hollings and probably had twice my experience of buying and selling modern first editions. I gave up all hope of a great bargain and went on steadily bidding up to about £300, when to my surprise Miller dropped out and the Henry James collection was knocked down to me.

The rather indifferent James books went into my stock but I decided to list *Guy Domville*, priced at £500, in my Catalogue 65 which was issued in October 1966. This catalogue contained some scarce books which had been in John Hayward's library, and other rare books from the collection of the bibliophile R. N. Green-Armytage, but none so rare as the James. I left *Guy Domville* until the end of the catalogue, describing it on two pages, as a kind of postscript, quoting the description of the book given in the bibliography by Edel and Laurence: 'Non-published edition . . . .. Five copies are known to be extant, one each in the Houghton, Huntington and Colby libraries, a fourth in the Lord Chamberlain's office, London, and a fifth in the collection of Mr. C. Waller Barrett . . . .' I mentioned that it was in a presentation binding, and was inscribed by the actor-manager of the play: 'To Henry Blyth with best wishes from George Alexander.' Catalogue 65 was issued on October 20, 1966, and on October 24 the book was bought by the Bodleian Library, I think at the suggestion of Simon Nowell-Smith, to whom all James enthusiasts must be grateful for his delightful book *The Legend of the Master*.

4. ————————ROSS MACDONALD: THE DARK BACKWARD

The books on my list of twenty favourite mystery novels would all be by American authors. I have never been interested in 'a classic closed community of suspects' or stories with trick endings or revelations on the last page. I want characters who come to life as you read, a sense of reality, atmosphere, emotion and excitement and I find them much more often in the suspense novels written on the other side of the Atlantic.

My list would begin with Dashiell Hammett's famous book *The Maltese Falcon* and include a number of other well known novels such as W.R. Burnett's *The Asphalt Jungle* (the filmed version of this, directed by John Huston, would be on my list of twenty favourite movies), Stanley Ellin's *The Eighth Circle*, William McGivern's *The Big Heat* (another favourite movie, with an unforgettable confrontation between Glenn Ford and Lee Marvin), George V. Higgins' *The Friends of Eddie Coyle* and *The Defection of A.J. Lewinter* by Robert Littell. But I should also include some crime novels which I believe have been unjustly neglected: Ira Wolfert's subtle book *Tucker's People* (again made into a brilliant movie called *Force of Evil*, starring John Garfield), Robert Knowlton's *Court of Crows*, Thomas Walsh's *Nightmare in Manhattan*, Eleazar Lipsky's *The People Against O'Hara* and Herbert Lieberman's *City of the Dead*. My list would end chronologically with Andrew Coburn's *Off Duty* but on grounds of merit it would be close to the top of the list.

Dashiell Hammett would be represented by two books on the list, *The Maltese Falcon* and *The Glass Key*. Ross Macdonald wrote, 'we all came out from under Hammett's black mask,' and for me Hammett is the Master. Any talented writer could base an interesting or amusing character on Hammett's famous 'fat man', but to create originals like Caspar Gutman ('the fat man was flabbily fat with bulbous pink cheeks and lips and chins and neck, with a great soft egg of a belly that was all his torso, and pendant cones for arms and legs'), Joel Cairo and Sam Spade takes more than talent. As Raymond Chandler wrote of Hammett, 'he wrote scenes that seemed never to have been written before.'

Chandler, too, would probably be represented by two books on the list but choosing them would be difficult. The problem is that I like parts of various books by Chandler very much indeed but two favourite titles do not spring to mind readily as they do with Hammett. And my critical judgement might well be influenced by my memories of the Chandler movies. I should find it very difficult to erase images of Humphrey Bogart as Philip Marlowe in *The Big Sleep*, sweating out his interview in the greenhouse with General Sternwood, fending off the foolish Carmen and grinning wolfishly at Mrs. Regan.

Reviewing my favourite suspense novels I see how many of them have one factor in common, that the mysteries stem from events that occurred way back in the past. In *The Tempest* Prospero asks Miranda, 'What seest thou else in the dark backward and abysm of time?' I must admit to being fascinated by the past and some friends might say that I am obsessed with it: old songs, old movies, old discs, old photographs and much else to do with 'all the dearly beloved,' all those human beings who have lived and died. In *The Maltese Falcon* the tricks, lies, treachery and violent deaths stem from the hunt for a 'foot-high jewelled bird': 'For seventy years, sir, this marvellous item was, as you might say, a football in the gutters of Paris—until 1911 when a Greek dealer named Charilaos Konstantinides found it in an obscure shop . . . .' And in Coburn's book *Off Duty* the foreground is taken up with a hi-jacked drugs deal, the involvement of the Boston mafia and the brutal killing of a man, flayed with a bunch of antique keys ('flayed by something that had removed flesh, big bits and pieces, and dislodged an eye'), but the ultimate source of all this violence is the simple fact that years before the two main characters, Rupert Goetz and Frank Chase, had been in love with the same woman.

Many of the books written by Ross Macdonald are bound up with events that took place in the past: his private detective Lew Archer sets out on what appears at first to be a relatively simple case, but the puzzle proves to be complex and leads Archer further and further back into the past. I have fourteen novels by Ross Macdonald on my shelves for favourite thrillers and I find it extremely difficult to select just two or three for my list.

A review of *The Moving Target* by 'John Macdonald' (Kenneth Millar's first pseudonym as an author) led me to buy the book within a few weeks of its publication in England in 1951, by Cassell in their 'Crime Connoisseur' series. I was attracted by the abrupt start: 'The cab turned off U.S. 101 in the direction of the sea. The road looped round the base of a brown hill into a canyon lined with scrub oak . . . .' Then I enjoyed the account of the detective Lew Arless's first meeting with his crippled client in Carillo Canyon: 'Mrs. Sampson looked up from her book . . . . She was half lying on a chaise longue with her back to the late morning sun, a towel draped over her body. There was a wheelchair standing beside her, but she didn't look like an invalid. She was very lean and brown, tanned so dark her flesh seemed hard. Her hair was bleached, curled tightly on her narrow head like blobs of whipped cream. Her age was as hard to tell as the age of a figure carved from mahogany.'

Mrs. Sampson's tart quips appealed to me. On two divorced friends: 'Millicent and Clyde are dreadfully sordid, don't you think? These aesthetic men! I've always suspected his mistress wasn't a woman.' Lew Arless is shown a photograph of Mr. Sampson, the missing millionaire husband: 'The face in the leather folder was fat, with thin grey hair and a troubled mouth. The thick nose tried to be bold and succeeded in being obstinate. The smile that folded the puffed eyelids and creased the sagging cheeks was fixed and forced. I'd seen such smiles in mortuaries on the false face of death. It reminded me that I was going to grow old and die.' Mrs. Sampson commented on it: 'A poor thing, but mine own.'

The wisecracks in *The Moving Target* seemed to me to be up to Raymond Chandler's high standard, but I thought that 'John Macdonald' could sometimes draw an even more telling vignette. In the second chapter there is a good example of this, a description of Miss Sampson (the missing man's daughter) and Alan Taggart (his pilot) together in a swimming pool: 'The pool was on the upper terrace, an oval of green water set in blue tile. A girl and a boy were playing tag, cutting the water like seals. The girl was chasing the boy. He let her catch him. Then they were a man and a woman, and the moving scene froze in the sun. Only the water moved, and the girl's hands. She was standing behind him with her arms round his waist. Her fingers moved over his ribs gently as a harpist's, clenched in the tuft of hair in the centre of his chest. Her face was hidden against his back. His face held pride and anger like a blind bronze. He pushed her hands down and stepped away. Her face was naked then and terribly vulnerable . . . .'

Minor characters are sketched in with economy but their images tend to remain in the mind. 'The Filipino servant moved unobtrusively across the patio. Felix's steady smile was a mask behind which his personality waited in isolation, peeping furtively from the depths of his bruised-looking eyes. I had the feeling that his pointed ears heard everything I said, counted my breathing, and could pick up the beat of my heart . . . .'

This is the description of Arless's first encounter with Puddler, an ex-boxer: 'The hand missed the bowl (of salted peanuts) and scrabbled in the grass like a crippled lobster. Then he turned his head, and I saw the side of his face . . . it wasn't the face the man in the scarlet shirt had started out with. It was a stone face hacked out by a primitive sculptor. It told a very common twentieth-century story: too many fights, too many animal guts, not enough brains . . . . He was no taller than I was, and he wasn't as wide as the door, but he gave that impression. He made me nervous, the way you feel talking to a strange bulldog on his master's property . . . . I didn't like the way he moved towards me. His left shoulder was forward and his chin in, as if every hour of his day was divided into twenty three-minute rounds . . . .' It is such writing that makes me endorse what Eudora Welty wrote of Ross Macdonald, that he had 'the perspective that comes of precise observation and irony.'

I also enjoyed the way in which the story moved about in California, from 'Santa Teresa' to Hollywood and Pacific Palisades, and that each time 'the scene was as vivid as paint.' Other minor characters depicted in Hollywood are real enough to walk off the page; a contract writer for Metro: 'An ex-reporter from Chicago who had sold his first novel to Metro and never written another, Hunt was turning from a hopeful kid to a nasty old man with the migraines and a swimming pool he couldn't use because he was afraid of the water. I had helped him lose his second wife to make way for his third, who was no improvement . . . .'

But the finest word portrait seemed to me to be that of the psychic, ageing film actress Fay Estabrook (played by Shelley Winters in the movie): ' . . . In her dowdy costume—black hat with a widow's veil and plain black coat—her big, handsome body looked awkward and ungainly. It may have been the sun in my eyes or simple romanticism, but I had the feeling that the evil which hung in the studio air like an odourless gas was concentrated in that heavy black figure wandering up the empty factitious street . . . . In the Hollywood Roosevelt bar she complained of the air and said she felt wretched and old. Nonsense, I told her, but we moved to the Zebra Room . . . . In the Zebra Room she accused the man at the next table of looking at her contemptuously. I suggested more air. She drove down Wilshire as if she was trying to break into another dimension . . .. She quarrelled with the Ambassador barman on the grounds that he laughed at her when he turned his back . . ... The lady passed out again. At least she said nothing. It was a lonely drive down the midnight boulevard with her half-conscious body. In the spotted coat it was like a sleeping animal beside me in the seat, a leopard or a wildcat heavy with age. It wasn't really old—fifty at most—but it was full of the years, full and fermenting with bad memories. She'd told me a number of things about herself, but not what I wanted to know, and I was too sick of her to probe deeper. The only sure thing I knew about her she hadn't had to tell me: she was bad company for Sampson or any incautious man. Her playmates were dangerous . . ..'

There is a really masterly scene where Arless deliberately gets Mrs. Estabrook drunk: 'The second drink fixed her. Her face went to pieces as if by its own weight. Her eyes were full and unblinking. Her mouth hung open in a fixed yawn, the scarlet lips contrasting with the pink-and-white interior. She brought it together numbly and whispered: "I don't feel so good." . . . The waitress held the door open with a condoling smile for Mrs. Estabrook and sharp glance for me. Mrs. Estabrook stumbled across the sidewalk like an old woman leaning on a cane that wasn't there. I held her up on her anaethetized legs . . ..'

And another brilliant scene takes place when Mrs. Estabrook passes out once more, when she is in her house, alone with Arless: ' "I can't think of anything I want to drink," she whined. "Don't let me fall." I put one arm round her shoulders, which were almost as wide as mine. She leaned hard against me. I felt the stir and swell of her breathing, gradually slowing down. "Don't try to do anything to me, honey, I'm dead tonight. Some other night . . .." Her voice was soft and somehow girlish, but blurred. Blurred like the submarine glints of youth in her eyes. Her eyes closed. I could see the faint tremor of her heart-beat in the veins of her withering eyelids. Their fringe of curved dark lashes was a vestige of youth and beauty which made her ruin seem final and hard. It was easier to feel sorry for her when she was sleeping. . ..'

So, *The Moving Target* is a 'must' for my list. It led to me tracking down the only other book then available by Kenneth Millar in Britain, *Blue City*, published by Cassell in 1949. Once more I was attracted by the deceptively simple opening paragraph: 'All the time you've been away from a town where you lived when you were a kid, you think about it and talk about it as if the air were sweeter in the nostrils than other air. When you meet a man from that town you feel a kind of brotherhood with him, till the talk runs down and you can't remember any more names.'

But though the descriptive writing in *Blue City* was effective the story seemed more stereotyped than *The Moving Target* and I found some of the violence (which led to a Bostonian critic describing it as 'Very, very tough. Not for delicate stomachs!') gratuitous so it will not find a place on my list.

More reluctantly I also pass over some of the early titles by 'John Ross Macdonald': *The Drowning Pool*, *The Way Some People Die*, *The Ivory Grin* and *Experience With Evil*. Along with the author's sensitivity, irony and descriptive powers I discerned in these books what the Germans call *Weltschmerz*, a sadness of the world, which I found sympathetic. More than most writers in the genre Ross Macdonald, in his essays, has put his finger on the attraction of such novels. He wrote: 'Perhaps, like Mithridates sampling his daily poison, we swallow our regular quotas of fictitious fear and danger in order to strengthen our minds against the real thing. Perhaps we need to be reminded that our planet is an uncertain and unsafe place . . . .'

Again while wearing his other hat, that of the perceptive essayist, Ross Macdonald wrote of the mystery novel writer: ' . . . he can lie in wait . . . against the day when another book will haunt him like a ghost rising out of both the past and the future.' *The Galton Case* (published by Cassell in 1960) begins in the late nineteen-fifties when the dying Mrs. Galton hires Lew Archer to find her long-lost son, Anthony. It has a simple but effective opening paragraph: 'The law offices of Wellesly and Sable were over a savings bank on the main street of Santa Teresa. Their private elevator lifted you from a bare little lobby into an atmosphere of elegant simplicity. It created the impression that after years of struggle you were rising effortlessly to your natural level, one of the chosen.'

The Galton case looks hopeless at the start and is described as such by the lawyer, Gordon Sable, who first interviews Archer, for the son had been missing for over twenty years: ' "The son's name is, or was, Anthony Galton. He dropped out of sight in 1936. He was twenty-two at the time, just out of Stanford . . ." ' Archer's comment is: ' "That's a long time ago." From where I sat, it was like a previous century.' But the book does not only deal with events that had taken place in 1936, it goes back yet another decade 'to the lawless twenties and the notorious Lempi gang.'

The Galton Case contains a dozen brief but brilliant descriptions of the characters that Lew Archer encounters on his quest: 'The houseman came up closer to me and smiled. His smile was wide and raw, like a dog's grin, and meaningless, except that it meant trouble. His face was seamed with the marks of the trouble-prone. He invited violence, as certain other people invited friendship.' And this is the description of Mr. Culotti, a car-dealer: 'A grey-haired man came out, looking cheaply gala in an ice-cream suit. His face was swarthy and pitted like an Epstein bronze, and its two halves didn't quite match. When I got closer to him, I saw that one of his brown eyes was made of glass. He looked permanently startled.'

The plot of *The Galton Case* is complicated and involves the discovery of a headless skeleton and 'the fabulous Galton rubies which disappeared with the runaway,' and a boy's claim to be the son of the missing Anthony Galton. But Ross Macdonald effortlessly draws all these threads together in what the Cassell blurb-writer justly called 'an intriguing and brilliantly worked out climax.' The book is a strong contender for my list.

I think however that *The Underground Man*, published in England by Collins in 1971, is an even stronger contender (Ross Macdonald wrote: '. . . detective fiction can remind us that we are all underground men making a brief transit from darkness to darkness.'). In this book Lew Archer is again involved in a case that reaches back into the past, 'a web of murder and extortion stretching back through fifteen years,' but it also contains a haunting description of a tragic fire that ravages a hillside community in Southern California.

The reader finds a subtle hint of what is to come in the opening paragraph: 'A rattle of leaves woke me some time before dawn. A hot wind was breathing in at the bedroom window. I got up and closed the window and lay in bed and listened to the wind.' The fifth paragraph contains another prophetic image: 'It was a bright September morning. The edge of the sky had a yellowish tinge like cheap paper darkening in the sunlight. There was no wind at all now, but I could smell the inland desert and feel its heat.'

Poetical descriptions of the fire paint a dramatic backcloth against which the mystery is solved: 'Sparks and embers were blowing down the canyon, plunging into the trees behind the house like bright exotic birds taking the place of the birds that had flown . . . . Smoke hung over the city, giving it a sepia tint like an old photograph. We climbed out of the cars and looked back at the house. The fire bent round it like the fingers of a hand, squeezing smoke out of the windows and then flames . . . . The hillside path was littered with black sticks and grey ashes . . . . I passed the place where the stable had been. The burned-out body of Stanley's convertible was sitting in the open, its tyreless rims sunk in the ashes of the building. It looked like a relic of an ancient civilization, ruined and diminished by the passage of centuries, already half buried among their droppings . . . .'

The fire scenes have the authenticity of hard won experience but they are rivalled by the word portraits of people. This is Mrs. Crandall, living in Pacific Palisades: ' . . . on a palm-lined street in a kind of Tudor manor with a peaked roof and brown obtruding half-timbers . . .. A blonde woman in black opened the ornately carved door. Her body was so trim against the light that I thought for a moment she was a girl. Then she inclined her head to look at me, and I saw that time had faintly touched her face and begun to tug at her throat . . .. Her speech was carefully correct, as if she had taken lessons in talking. I suspected that her natural speech was a good deal rougher and freer. Her body fell into a beautiful still pose, but her faintly pinched face seemed bored with it, or resentful, like an angel living with an animal.'

And this is her husband: 'Lester Crandall came into the room as if he was the visitor, not I. He was a short heavy-bodied man with iron grey hair and sideburns which seemed to pincer his slightly crumpled face and hold it for inspection. His smile was that of a man who wanted to be liked. His handshake was firm and I noticed that his hands were large and misshapen. They bore the old marks of heavy work: swollen knuckles, roughened skin. He had spent his life, I thought, working his way to the top of a small hill which his daughter had abandoned in one jump. He was like a man with his eyes closed trying to put his hands on a girl that wasn't there. I began to think I had a glimmering of the problem. It was often the same problem—an unreality so bland and smothering that the children tore loose and impaled themselves on the spikes of any reality that offered. Or made their own unreality with drugs.'

I also have to include *The Blue Hammer* (the last Ross Macdonald mystery novel, published in England by Collins in 1976) on my list. Lew Archer is hired by Ruth Biemeyer, the wife of a copper magnate, to find a stolen painting, but really he has to solve a number of mysteries and—gradually—'Is drawn into a web of family complications and masked brutalities stretching back fifty years through a world where money talks or buys silence . . . .' The stolen canvas was the work of an artist Richard Chantry who had himself been missing for 25 years when the story opens. At one point Archer says, 'This case was started in 1943. It's time it was closed . . ..'

This is the author's description of one locale: 'The University had been built on an elevated spur of land that jutted the sea and was narrowed at its base by a tidal slough. Almost surrounded by water and softened by blue haze, it looked from the distance like a medieval fortress town. Close up, the buildings shed this romantic aspect. They were half-heartedly modern, cubes and oblongs and slabs that looked as if the architect had spent his life designing business buildings . . . .'

A number of the descriptions, written in a few lines, are as effective as Imagist poems: ' . . . I could see the harbour in the distance. Its masts and cordage resembled a bleached winter grove stripped of leaves and gauntly beautiful. The candle flames reflected in the windows seemed to flicker like St. Elmo's fire around the distant masts. Below the house the sea thumped and fumbled like a dead man trying to climb back into life. I shivered . . . .'

In *The Blue Hammer* the author's comments on men and women seem to me like the distillation of a lifetime largely spent in trying to understand them: 'Looking into Paolo's opaque black eyes, I thought that the grief you share with women was most always partly desire. At least sometimes you could take them to bed, I thought, and exchange a temporary kindness, which priests were denied . . . . My chosen study was other men, hunted men in rented rooms, ageing boys clutching at manhood before night fell and they grew suddenly old. If you were the therapist, how could you need therapy? If you were the hunter, you couldn't be hunted. Or could you? She tapped the floor with her toe, and her whole body moved. She was one of those women whose sex had aged into artiness but might still flare up if given provocation . . . . She moved to unlatch the outer door. Until then, she hadn't shown her age. She was lame, and her hips moved awkwardly. I was reminded of certain kinds of pelagic birds that moved at ease in the air or on the ocean, but have a hard time walking. Her white head was like a bird's. It was sparse and elegant, with hollow cheeks, a thin straight nose, eyes that still had distance and wildness. She caught me looking at her, and smiled. One of her front teeth was missing. It gave her a gamine touch.'

The plot of *The Blue Hammer* is extremely complicated, perhaps too much so to be readily followed, and this leads to a kind of Dickensian ploy in Chapter XLI where Lew Archer recapitulates: 'I sat in my car in the failing afternoon and tried to straighten out the case in my mind. It had started with the trouble between two brothers, Richard Chantry and his illegitimate half-brother. It appeared that Richard had stolen William's work and William's girl . . . .' Despite this complexity the reader is carried along by the author's skill and some brilliant scenes, like the one in the following chapter in which Archer confronts Mrs. Chantry: 'Francine had been living for decades deep in the knowledge of murder. It was beginning to show in her face and body, reaching up for her from the earth like gravity . . . . Her jaw was slack and grim, her eyes dull. But she held on to her bag the way a plunging fullback holds the ball . . . . "Were you in an accident?" "I don't really know what happened. I was trying to get off the freeway, and things went out of control all of a sudden. That seems to be the story of my life." Her laughter was like a dry compulsive cough . . . there was a note of terror in Francine Chantry's voice. She sounded like a woman who had stepped off the edge of the world and discovered too late that she could never step back. When we got into my car and entered the freeway, the sense of moving through empty space stayed with me. We seemed to be flying above the rooftops of the tract houses that lined the freeway on both sides . . . .'

No, I can't relinquish *The Blue Hammer* as a favourite mystery novel but neither can I discard *The Moving Target*, *The Galton Case* or *The Underground Man*—so I must re-plan my list to make room for four titles by Ross Macdonald.

5. —— *REX V. PEMBERTON-BILLING*

After his close involvement with the three trials of Oscar Wilde in 1895 Lord Alfred Douglas seems to have developed a complex about the Law. Perhaps appearances in Court appealed to an innate sense of theatricality or provided an outlet for the trait of aggression which he undoubtedly inherited from his father John Sholto, the notorious Marquess of Queensberry, who liked to consort with pugilists and often behaved aggressively, attacking another son, Percy, in the street on 21 May 1895. Certainly Alfred Douglas appeared to enjoy the dubious limelight that legal cases bring with them. In 1912 he issued writs for libel against Arthur Ransome, Martin Secker and The Times Book Club; in 1913 he appeared in Court for criminally libelling his father-in-law, Colonel Custance, while at the same time being involved in a Chancery Court case over the custody of his son, Raymond; in 1914 he was on trial again for libelling Robert Ross who, in a relatively short period, had been transformed from a close friend to a bête noire; and over a period of years he recklessly published pamphlets libelling numerous people until 1923 when he was brought to trial for libelling Winston Churchill—an escapade which led to him serving a six-month sentence in Wormwood Scrubs Prison. But none of these cases was as curious and complicated as the 1918 Noel Pemberton-Billing trial in which Douglas appeared as an enthusiastic supporter and witness for Billing. This case, sometimes known as the 'Black Book' trial, was like the box which Zeus gave to Pandora, for what appeared to be a relatively simple libel case was in fact a most complex matter masking a Major-General's concern about secret peace negotiations, fanatical anti-Semitism, and Billing's claim that there was a pro-German Fifth Column at work in England.

When Noel Pemberton-Billing died at the age of sixty-eight in 1948
he was a largely forgotten man and the Press made little of his death, but
he had been a colourful personality and multi-talented which led to him
becoming a pilot, actor, business man, inventor, sailor, publicist, playwright
and Member of Parliament. While still a young man Billing founded the
Supermarine Aircraft Company and served in the Royal Naval Air Service
until 1916 when he resigned his commission as a Squadron Leader in order
to stand for Parliament. This was at a time when the Royal Family abandoned
its foreign titles and their name was changed from Wettin to Windsor. Billing
also founded the Vigilante Society 'to promote purity in public life and root
out mysterious influences in England.' This kind of thing appealed to Alfred
Douglas who had publicly attacked Herbert Asquith, then Prime Minister,
and his wife in a libellous sonnet entitled 'All's Well With England':

> Out there in Flanders all the trampled ground
> Is red with English blood, our children pass
> Through fire to Moloch. Who will count the cost,
> Since here "at home" sits merry Margot, bound
> With Lesbian fillets, while with front of brass
> "Old Squiffy" hands the purse to Robert Ross?

To spread his propaganda Billing started a newspaper called the
Imperialist, having found a number of like-minded men as contributors
including a Captain Spencer who had been dismissed from the British Secret
Service as insane, and the sinister Dr. J.H. Clarke who specialized in racial
hatred. A third colleague was the violently anti-Semitic H.H. Beamish who
said that the German Jews, the *Ashkenazim*, had infiltrated all levels of the
ruling classes. Their creed found another spokesman in Billing's friend
Arnold White, editor of the *English Review*, who believed in forced Jewish
colonisation in Argentina.

On 26 January 1918 Billing published a major article in the *Imperialist*:

The First 47,000

There have been many reasons why England is prevented from putting
her full strength into the War. Hope of profit cannot be the only reason
for our betrayal. All nations have their Harlot on the Wall, but . . .
it is in the citadel that true danger lies. Corruption and blackmail, being
the work of menials, is cheaper than bribery. Moreover fear of exposure
entraps and makes slaves of men whom money could never buy . . . .
There exists in the *Cabinet noir* of a certain German Prince a book
compiled by the Secret Service from the reports of German agents who

have infested this country for the past twenty years, agents so vile and spreading debauchery of such a lasciviousness as only German minds could conceive and only German bodies execute.

The officer who discovered this book while on special service briefly outlined for me its stupefying contents which all decent men thought had perished in Sodom and Lesbia . . ..

The article went on to state that the book of more than a thousand pages listed the names of 47,000 English men and women who had been the subjects of the German reports: 'It is a most catholic miscellany. The names of Privy Councillors, youths of the chorus, wives of Cabinet Ministers, dancing girls, even Cabinet Ministers themselves . . . .' On 2 February 1918 the last issue of the *Imperialist* appeared; it included an attack on the 'Shylocks from Frankfurt.' The following week the same paper appeared with a new name, the *Vigilante*. On the day following the publication of the *Vigilante* there was an announcement in the *Sunday Times* that two private performances of Oscar Wilde's play *Salomé* were to be given privately for subscribers to a theatrical group at a London theatre on 7 and 14 April. The producer was to be J. T. Grein, a businessman who ran the Independent Theatre; the actress he had chosen to play Salomé was Maud Allan.

Marie Corelli, the best-selling romantic novelist, saw this announcement in the *Sunday Times* and sent it to Billing with a short note:

Dear Mr. Billing,

I think it would be well to secure a list of subscribers to the new "upholding" of the Wilde "cult" among the 47,000.

Yours sincerely,
Marie Corelli

P.S. Why "private" performances?

Billing's next step was reckless in that he printed something manifestly obscene. On the front page of the *Vigilante* of 16 February 1918 this appeared:

The Cult of the Clitoris

To be a member of Maud Allan's private performances in Oscar Wilde's Salomé one has to apply to a Miss Valetta, of 9, Duke Street, Adelphi, W.C. If Scotland Yard were to seize the list of these members I have no doubt they would secure the names of several thousand of the first 47,000 . . ..

When this startling announcement was made, some of Billing's friends were worried that he might have gone too far and laid himself open to criminal proceedings by the Director of Public Prosecutions; but at the same time events in the War led to him gaining other, secret allies. Major-General Sir Frederick Maurice, who was General Robertson's Director of Military Operations, was convinced that the Government's policy for fighting the war was 'fundamentally wrong and leading to disaster.' General Maurice sought support in the Press for his views and went to Lt-Colonel Charles à Court Repington of *The Times*. Repington was an influential writer on the war, but also an embittered man because his own army career had foundered through his affair with a married woman in Cairo. By 1918 his reputation as a writer was at its height but his visits to Haig's GHQ in France were not altogether welcome. 'Repington is a law unto himself, overweeningly conceited, and with a dulled sense of honour,' wrote Haig's Intelligence Officer. General Maurice approached Repington two days after his resignation from *The Times* and just before his appointment as War Correspondent to the ultra-conservative *Morning Post*; he hoped that Repington would provide him with a platform for public attacks on Lloyd George and the conduct of the war. And it appears that, in turn, Repington approached Billing with the idea of support for his views from the *Morning Post*; the editor of that paper was then H.A. Gwynne, another virulent anti-Semite.

On 5 March Jack Grein saw the offensive paragraph that had been published in the *Vigilante* and showed it to Maud Allan. They both went to their solicitors to consult them about a libel action against Billing. On 8 March Grein and Maud Allan appeared before Mr. Judge Salter in Chambers seeking permission to start criminal proceedings for both criminal and obscene libel against Billing. As they had not been able to obtain a copy of the *Imperialist* for 26 January, Counsel for the Prosecution asked leave to start proceedings on the five words in the title of the offending paragraph, 'The Cult of the Clitoris.' Billing skillfully objected to this and the Judge adjourned the matter. On 24 March the solicitors acting for Grein and Maud Allan managed to obtain a copy of the issue of *Imperialist* and a summons was served on Billing.

On 21 March the Germans, under General von Ludendorf, began their last major offensive of the war, an attack falling mainly on the British Army. The rout of the British was so serious that the War Cabinet talked of pulling the troops back to the Channel ports. Anxiety over this perilous situation in the minds of some British Generals was mixed with disquiet over the rumours of secret peace talks with the German Foreign Minister, Richard von Kühlmann.

Salomé was performed on 12 April at the Court Theatre, prefaced by a statement—a 'Tribute to Britain'—by Grein in which he stated that the play was 'not an impure work.' The performance received some hostile reviews and the *Morning Post* described it as 'a bizarre melodrama of disease.'

The trial of Noel Pemberton-Billing MP began on 29 May 1918, and it should be remembered that by that date the Germans were approaching Paris and the trial was conducted against a background of general war anxiety and hysteria. It was held at the Old Bailey before Mr. Justice Darling. Mr. Hume-Williams K.C., Mr. Travers Humphreys and Mr. J.P. Valetta appeared for the prosecution. The colourful defendant (who wore a monocle and drove a canary-coloured Rolls Royce) decided to conduct his own defence. Since Billing was pleading Not Guilty he had to submit in writing the details of justification to the Court. He wrote: 'The tragedy of *Salomé* is a stage play by one Oscar Wilde, a moral pervert . . . an open representation of degenerated sexual lust, sexual crime, and unnatural passions and an evil and mischievous travesty of a biblical story . . . .' He further declared that 'the German authorities, in furtherance of their hostile designs upon this country, have for some years past by means of spies and secret agents, and otherwise, compiled a list of men and women of various social, political, financial and other positions and occupations in this country with a record of their alleged moral, sexual and other weaknesses, and with all the information procurable concerning which would render such persons easy victims of pressure, and enable them under fear of threats of exposure to be forced into courses of conduct agreeable to the wishes of German agents in this country and of their superiors in Germany.'

Fireworks started early on in the proceedings when Billing, in true Alfred Douglas style, began with an attack on the Judge. He protested that Mr. Justice Darling should not be trying the case because in Billing's position as a public man and Member of Parliament he had often criticized Darling's administration of justice in the Press. Darling dismissed this suggestion.

In an opening speech for the prosecution Hume-Williams said that the statement about Maud Allan in the *Vigilante* was 'a libel of such a gross kind, so outrageous in form, that the proceedings came within the purview of the criminal law instead of a civil action being brought.' Showing that his mode of defence was to be, like the French cavalry, 'attack—always attack,' Billing forced Maud Allan to admit that her brother had been executed for murdering two young girls. Despite this low blow Miss Allan proved to be a spirited witness, holding her own with Billing in a number of exchanges.

As his first witness for the defence Billing produced a Mrs. Eileen Villiers Stuart and persisted in asking her questions which were inadmissible. When reproved Billing stated, 'I know nothing about evidence and I know nothing about the law. I came to this Court in the public interest to prove what I propose to prove.' Mr. Justice Darling's succinct reply was, 'Very well, then you must prove it according to the ordinary rules of evidence.'

Lord Alfred Douglas was called by the defendant as an expert witness and the translator of the play, which had originally been written in French. He gave his 1918 verdict on Wilde, that he was 'the greatest force for evil that has appeared in Europe during the last three hundred and fifty years.' Douglas also said that he intensely regretted having met Wilde and helping him with the translation which he presently regarded as 'a most pernicious and abominable piece of work.'

By 30 May 1918 the Germans had reached the river Marne and were present in large numbers between the Marne and the Aisne; the position on the Western Front was therefore regarded as being critical. Despite this dramatic position, both for France and the British Army, a lot of space in the Press was given to the Pemberton-Billing trial, and the Old Bailey courtroom was crowded. Alfred Douglas received some vocal support when he turned on Mr. Justice Darling, before whom he had previously appeared in 1913; when cross-examined by Hume-Williams about the notorious 'prose poem' written to him by Wilde, Douglas protested 'every time I come here this bestial drivel is brought up . . .. You ought to be ashamed to bring it out here.' Darling ruled that Douglas could not comment on counsel and Douglas excitedly replied, 'I shall answer the questions as I please. I came here to give my evidence. You bullied me at the last trial, I shall not be bullied and brow-beaten by you again. You deliberately lost me my case in the last trial . . ..' Darling then threatened Douglas with removal from court and there was another rejoinder which was greeted by a burst of cheering from some of the spectators in the gallery. When Douglas was removed from the court he shouted out, 'You have no right to say that I wrote it. You lie. You are a liar, a damned liar. If you say it outside the court I will prosecute you.' He left the court on this dramatic note but a few minutes later provoked laughter when he begged leave to return to retrieve his top hat which he had left behind in his hurried exit.

On the fifth day of the trial Billing made some good points in his defence, and others that were irrelevant but very popular with the audience in the court: 'Gentlemen of the Jury, I assure you that there must be some reason for all the "regrettable incidents" of this war . . ... What is the

position in France today? It is worse than it was in August 1914. The best
of the blood in this country is already spilled; and do you think I am going
to keep quiet in my position as a public man while nine men die in a minute
to make a sodomite's holiday?'

It was also on the fifth day of the trial that Billing defended Douglas:
'I bring Lord Alfred Douglas into that box, a man who was led down the
valley of vice by the very man who wrote this play. I admire Lord Alfred's
courage in coming here. The story of his regrettable past almost forgotten;
wiped out and washed out by the conflagration of Europe . . . he comes
back into the witness-box . . . knowing full well that they would rake up
the whole of that sordid and regrettable past, he came here. And they raked
it up. The leader of the Prosecution stood up and licked his lips with
satisfaction as he read out all the sordid filth written to that child—the love
letters of Oscar Wilde who ruined him, read against him as something for
which he ought to have been ashamed. They may try to hurl mud at the
witnesses I have brought here; but it is no use bringing people here who
have never heard of sodomy, who have never heard of sadism . . . .'

On the sixth and final day of the trial Billing and Mr. Justice Darling
had a number of fiery exchanges, one of them being over Viscount Grey:

> JUDGE: The matter I regretted more than anything else was to have
> the name of Viscount Grey introduced into such a case as
> this—filled with impurity from one end to the other. I should
> have thought if there was a man in England whose character
> . . . could not be mentioned in such a case as this, it would
> have been Viscount Grey . . . .

BILLING: I never mentioned the name of Sir Edward Grey.
JUDGE: Your witness did.
BILLING: No, my Lord.
JUDGE: Your witness said so in the box.
A VOICE: Never, my Lord.
JUDGE: Turn that man out of court at once.

The jury in the Central Criminal Court retired at 3.15 pm and returned
at 4.40 pm. They brought in a verdict of Not Guilty and there was
pandemonium in the court with the packed gallery rising to their feet,
shouting and cheering—a veritable storm of applause accompanied by
stamping feet. The Judge ordered everyone out of the gallery. After Billing
had been discharged he continued to show panache by rising to his feet and
making another request:

BILLING: My Lord—
JUDGE: You have nothing to say, sir. You are discharged.
BILLING: My Lord, I beg formally to apply for the costs of these
        proceedings.
JUDGE: You are discharged.

It is said that Mr. Justice Darling left the court white and visibly shaken by Billing's effrontery.

A crowd of thousands outside the Old Bailey greeted Noel Pemberton-Billing as he descended the steps of the main entrance. In response to their cheers he waved his hat repeatedly until the police were able to clear the way for his yellow Rolls Royce. Lord Alfred Douglas was similarly greeted, and he shouted, 'It is splendid, splendid.'

Basil Thomson, the Assistant Commissioner of Police, noted in his diary his conclusion that everyone concerned with the trial appeared to be insane. On 4 June 1918 he wrote: 'One might treat the case with contempt, were it not for its pernicious influence throughout this and neutral countries . . . .'

The newspapers on 5 June bore headlines such as 'SUPREME WAR COUNCIL CONFIDENT — ENEMY ATTACK SLACKEN-ING — AMERICAN COUNTERATTACK.' The *Manchester Guardian* was very critical of Billing: 'No-one has ever thrown so much dirt on people more respected than himself, and yet come so near to being a local hero. Few people have made such a miasma and escaped punishment for creating a public nuisance . . . .'

The Times had a first leader with a headline 'A Scandalous Trial': ' . . . no lawsuit of modern times has attracted such universal and painful interest as the deplorable libel action which terminated yesterday at the Central Criminal Court. Not only in London, but even more in the provincial towns and countryside, the daily reports have been read and discussed with almost as deep anxiety as the news of the war itself . . . .'

The *Daily Mail* also had a leading article on the Billing case, arguing that the verdict was not based on the evidence presented to the court and that Billing had hardly bothered to deal with the actual counts on which he had been indicted: 'He brought forward, instead, a vast deal of hearsay testimony more appropriate to Bedlam or to a Drury Lane melodrama than to a British court of justice . . . . The proceedings in court constituted in this respect nothing less than a libel on the nation . . . . Scenes were enacted of such grotesque unseemliness that the court at times resembled a madhouse . . . .' The paper's verdict on Mr. Justice Darling was that he had been faced with a difficult task 'but he failed most lamentably to grapple with it.'

Attacks in the Press left Noel Pemberton-Billing, Independent MP for East Hertfordshire, quite unperturbed. On 9 June 1918, when the Hague Conference opened, he wrote a major article for a Sunday paper headed 'My Fight for a Cleaner England—The Hidden Hand of the Hun.'

6. —— *HARLEY GRANVILLE BARKER*

It was the BBC productions, in 1960, of some of Harley Granville Barker's plays which first stimulated my interest in his writings. I have never been a theatre-goer and rarely read plays, but the broadcast versions of *The Voysey Inheritance*, *Waste*, *The Madras House*, and particularly *The Secret Life* appealed to me strongly. I soon obtained the texts of the plays, and C.B. Purdom's biography of H.G.B. which had been published in 1955; I also made notes on the plays and the author. George Sampson wrote that *The Secret Life* (1919-1923): ' . . . is a puzzling, disturbing post-war play that shows us the intellectual world reduced to a spiritual nihilism. There is no clear centre of dramatic interest. The characters just come and go, and what "love interest" there is seems entirely gratuitous. The dialogue is sometimes normally dramatic, sometimes philosophically enigmatic, as if the speakers had no other purpose than to ask riddles to which there can be no answer. Perhaps in no other volume is there so complete a revelation of the spiritual bankruptcy produced by the war.' George Moore was convinced that *The Secret Life* was Barker's finest play and C.B. Purdom wrote: 'It is, indeed, a striking work, one of the most beautifully written plays of the present century.'

By a lucky coincidence, in 1960 J.D. Miller, a bookseller operating from an office in Worthing, offered for sale some of Granville Barker's books which had come from the collection of Lady Keeble, formerly the actress Lillah McCarthy and Barker's first wife. On hearing from Miller that he was buying a good deal of this material, I made a number of visits to Worthing and purchased most of the items for sale then. That is the reason why many of the catalogues I issued in the 1960s contain so much unique Granville Barker material.

Harley Granville Barker was born on 25 November 1877 at 3A Sheffield Terrace in the Notting Hill area of West London. His father Arthur James Barker was a property dealer who became engaged in the disposal of land on the Howard de Walden estate. His mother Mary Elisabeth Bozzi-Granville was of Italian/Cornish descent. Little is known of Barker's early years because he never wrote about his parents, or his childhood and youth. His mother gave recitals of poetry on tours managed by her husband, and H.G.B. accompanied her on some of them.

It was in the spring of 1891 that Barker first appeared on the stage in the role of Dr. Grimstone in the play *Vice Versa*, and later that year he was sent to Sarah Thorne's theatrical school in Margate, Kent, but he only stayed there for a few months. The following year he had parts in two plays by Charles Brookfield. Afterwards he played parts for touring companies, and it was in Ben Greet's company that he first met Lillah McCarthy who was to become his wife. He also started writing plays in collaboration with Berte Thomas: *A Comedy of Fools*, *The Family of the Oldroyds*, and *The Weatherhen* of which a matinée performance was given at Terry's Theatre on 29 June 1899. It was during the late 1890s that he made a number of friends like William Archer, William Poel and Gilbert Murray who were to play important roles in developing his theatrical career.

On 29 April 1900 Granville Barker first became a producer for the Stage Society at the Globe Theatre, and early in the summer of that year he played Eugene in Shaw's play *Candida*, and a long and very fruitful relationship with G.B.S. began. Soon after they met Shaw wrote to the playwright Henry Arthur Jones: 'How do you get on with Granville Barker? Do you realize that he is a great poet and dramatist who feels towards us as we feel towards Sheridan Knowles?' As an old man Shaw gave his final verdict on Barker: 'He had a strong strain of Italian blood in him, and looked as if he had stepped out of a picture by Benozzo Gonzoli. He had a wide literary culture and a fastidiously delicate taste in every branch of art. He could write in a too precious but exquisitely fine style. He was self-willed, restlessly industri-ous, sober and quite sane. He had Shakespeare and Dickens at his finger ends. Altogether the most distinguished and incomparably the most cultivated person whom circumstances had driven into the theatre at that time.'

Barker took a room at 8 York Buildings, one reason for this being its closeness to Shaw's house in the Adelphi; he often visited the Shaws, both in London and at their country house in Herts. In December 1900 H.G.B.

appeared as Captain Kearney in Shaw's play *Captain Brassbound's Conversion* and then played the part of Napoleon in *The Man of Destiny*, also by G.B.S. Barker's own first play to be properly produced was *The Marrying of Ann Leete*, performed at the Royalty Theatre in January, 1902. Shaw called it 'really an exquisite play,' but it was damned by A.B. Walkley in *The Times*.

In 1902 Barker played the part of Osric in *Hamlet* and then the leading role in Maugham's play *A Man of Honour*. In his book *The Summing Up*, which appeared thirty-five years later, Maugham wrote: ' . . . Granville Barker was very young; I was only twenty-eight, and he, I think, was a year younger. He had charm and gaiety and coltish grace. He was brimming over with other people's ideas. But I felt in him a fear of life which he sought to cheat by contempt of the common herd. It was difficult to find anything he did not despise. He lacked spiritual vitality. I thought that an artist needed more force, more go, more bluntness, more guts, more beef.'

An important stage role for Barker was the name part in Marlowe's *Edward II*. A newspaper (*The Pilot*, 15 August 1903) paid this tribute to his acting: 'Mr. Granville Barker, one of the very cleverest of the younger generation, deserves much praise for his careful study of the King. In all the earlier scenes, arrogant, captious, self-willed, utterly regardless of his duties and the rights of others, and markedly epicene, he is as complete and truthful a figure as could be imagined . . . .'

It was at this time that Barker's dreams of, and obsession with, a National Theatre began, but some of his own stage performances were considered outstanding. When he appeared as Marchbanks in Shaw's *Candida*, Desmond MacCarthy wrote: 'Mr. Granville Barker succeeded in playing Eugene Marchbanks where almost every other actor would have failed, because the representation of a lyrical mood is one within the peculiar range of his powers . . . . It is in the representation of intellectual emotions that he excels, and so he excels in this part . . . .' Of his acting at this time Shaw wrote to Henry Arthur Jones: ' . . . always useful when a touch of poetry and refinement is needed. He can lift a whole cast when his part gives him a chance . . . .'

Despite his success Barker did not like acting and was anxious to change his role in the theatre. In 1904 there was an opportunity to do this in his partnership with J.E. Vedrenne and the management of the Royal Court Theatre, of which C.B. Purdom wrote: 'No theatrical company has left a deeper mark upon the theatrical history of London . . . .' Vedrenne was an astute business man whose talent married with that of H.G.B. in a very successful way. The theatre they chose had been built in 1888, on a site adjoining Sloane Square station on the Metropolitan railway; it seated 614 people and was a pleasant little theatre though not exactly in the West End. The new management's first production was Gilbert Murray's version of *Hippolytus* by Euripides, of which six matinées were given in October, 1904, followed by Shaw's play *John Bull's Other Island*, in which Barker played Keegan. This was declared an outstanding event and Mrs. Sidney Webb persuaded the Prime Minister, A.J. Balfour, to see it; Balfour so enjoyed it that he brought the Leader of the Opposition, Sir Henry Campbell-Bannerman, on a second visit and H.H. Asquith on a third! Barker suggested Lillah McCarthy for a part in the play and Shaw wrote to her: 'Can you talk real broad Irish, like Miss O'Malley in *John Bull's Other Island*? We cannot get her for the evening performance of that play (have you seen it?) in May. If Tree has not snapped you up for the rest of the season in the evenings, I should like to know whether you know the play and whether it attracts you at all . . . .' Henceforth Lillah McCarthy's life and stage career was to be bound up with Barker and Shaw. She wrote in her memoirs: ' . . . a new life began for me; a new life of the Court Theatre and of the new woman . . . .'

On 1 May 1905 a partnership agreement between Vedrenne and Barker was signed: it was to last for three years and then become subject to six months' notice by either partner. It is generally considered that this management's high-water mark was reached with their production of Shaw's *Man and Superman* in which Barker, made up to look like G.B.S., played John Tanner and Lillah McCarthy appeared as Ann Whitefield; the splendid cast also included Florence Haydon as Mrs. Whitefield, Lewis Casson and Edmund Gwenn.

The first of Granville Barker's important plays, *The Voysey Inheritance*, on which he had worked for two years, was produced on 7 November 1905, and was hailed as a masterpiece of the new drama. A.B. Walkley wrote that it had: ' . . . great merits. It has fresh and rare observation, subtle discrimination of character, sub-acid humour, an agreeable irony, and a general air of reality. That is the important thing.' Max Beerbohm's review was equally enthusiastic: 'Mr. Barker is an exceptional person, in whose presence I bow . . . . On him, somehow, the blight of the theatre has not fallen . . . . May his bright intellect never grow dim. I may have to suggest anon that he is too purely intellectual to be perfect. For the present, though, let there be nothing but praise.' Seven years later William Archer wrote, in *The Old Drama and the New*: 'I submit that, in *The Voysey Inheritance*, we have an English family group presented with a mastery of draughtsmanship and a depth of colour that remind us of a canvas of Rembrandt or Franz Hals, while at the same time the dramatic movement is sustained with subtle and original art . . . .'

It was at this time that Granville Barker's friendship with John Masefield began. Theodore Stier, who was then music director at the Court Theatre, wrote an account of Masefield's introduction there in his book of reminiscences *With Pavlova Round the World*: ' . . . a slim, poorly dressed and very shy young seaman insinuated himself through the door of my sanctum. "Mr. Barker told me to come and whistle to you," he said diffidently, twirling his cap in his hands . . . .. The young sailor went through the tunes that in his spare time he had composed in the fore-castle of a wooden sailing ship. When he got up to go, obviously relieved that his ordeal was at an end, I asked him his name. "John Masefield".' That encounter at the Court Theatre filled Masefield with ambition and within a year he was writing to Barker about the production of his first play, *The Campden Wonder*.

Lillah McCarthy and Harley Granville Barker were married on 24 April 1906 at the West Strand Registry Office, with no friends in attendance, and the marriage was kept secret from everyone except Shaw and Vedrenne. After a honeymoon in Germany and the Tyrol they went to live at 3 Clement's Inn, and later rented a cottage at Fernhurst, near Haslemere in Surrey. Lillah insisted that they should have a country retreat for Barker's health's sake and so that he could have somewhere to write undisturbed.

A complimentary dinner for Barker and Vedrenne was held at the Criterion Restaurant on 7 July 1907; 150 friends assembled for the event with Lord Lytton in the chair. Lytton concluded his speech by saying he hoped that they would be meeting again before long 'to congratulate our two guests of tonight on the completion of their experiment in the establishment of a real National Repertory Theatre.' In the same year the partnership took a lease on the Savoy Theatre in the Strand from Mrs. D'Oyley Carte. Shaw put up £2000 at 5 per cent interest to enable the Savoy season to begin but turned down the offer of becoming a partner in the venture. Under this new arrangement Vedrenne and Barker were to draw salaries of £1000 a year. Shaw said, 'My own salary, another thousand, is to be taken out in moral superiority.'

In the autumn of 1907 Barker learnt that his new play, *Waste*, was banned: the censor wanted a number of alterations; in particular all references to abortion were to be left out. A curious (technically public, but actually semi-private) performance of the play was given at 11 a.m. on 28 January 1908, in order to secure copyright, with a number of the author's friends including Gilbert Cannan, Laurence Housman, Gilbert Murray and H.G. Wells taking parts. There is no doubt that the play's political setting had a lot to do with the play being censored. There is a political thread in most of his plays and Margery Morgan's study of them is called *A Drama of a Political Man*.

The Vedrenne/Barker management virtually ended with the Savoy season which led to financial disaster and G.B. Shaw taking a heavy financial loss.

Early in 1908 the Barkers purchased the lease-hold of a small Elizabethan house called Court Lodge at Stansted in Kent. Granville Barker was now devoting much of his time to writing, and another important play, *The Madras House*, was first performed in a Charles Frohman repertory season at the Duke of York's Theatre, on 9 March 1910. John Masefield called it: 'very noble and very beautiful.' Max Beerbohm wrote: 'Every character in the play is a true study made by a man with a lust for accurate observation, and with an immense talent for sympathy.' Purdom wrote: 'In the sheer brilliance of its writing, the play is remarkable, one astounding act following another. Although the dialogue appears to be inconsequential, it has direct bearing upon the developing situation, and does more than merely create atmosphere: it contains the action . . . .'

Early in 1911 the Barkers took a small flat over the Little Theatre and, with the financial backing of Lord Howard de Walden, Lillah took a lease on the theatre itself. Plays produced there included *The Twelve-Pound Look* by J.M. Barrie, Ibsen's *The Master Builder* and Barker's *Rococo*. As part of the Coronation ceremonies the Prime Minister invited the Barkers to stage a performance at 10 Downing Street for the entertainment of King George V and Queen Mary.

Barker was spending most of his time at Stansted writing, but he was tempted back to the theatre as producer-manager for performances of Thomas Hardy's epic *The Dynasts* in December, 1914. Desmond MacCarthy called him 'the best producer of his time'—an opinion echoed by A.E. Matthews and other actors.

It was at the end of 1914 that Barker was invited to New York by the Stage Society. Among the millionaires who guaranteed the cost of an American season were Otto Kahn and Archer Huntington. Barker's meeting with Helen Huntington was to change his life because they fell in love and an affair began. During 1915 there was a period when Lillah hoped that the affair might be over but on 3 January 1916 she received a letter from Barker, written in New York, saying that he would not return to her and that she must divorce him. Shaw was in an awkward position, being friends with both husband and wife. On 19 January 1916 he wrote to Lillah: 'Quite seriously, I have come to the conclusion that you had better get rid of Harley. He has gone to France; and I have now no belief that you and he will ever patch it up again. If I am right, then the sooner you set yourself free the better for you, and the more creditable for him, as you are now at the height of your powers, and not soured or aged by your disagreement with him. I don't know whether either of you is to blame, or, if either, which; and it doesn't matter anyhow; but it seems to me that if you come together again you are more likely to drive one another mad than to settle down happily . . . .' Shaw wrote Lillah two more long letters advising her as best he could.

At this time Barker was nominally serving with the Red Cross but, like his later commission in the army, it seems to have been a tenuous arrangement which gave him a lot of freedom. He did compile a book titled *The Red Cross in France*. When he left that organization Barker returned to America and wrote a novella called *Souls on Fifth: The Slight Study of an American Hereafter*, published in New York in 1917, with a coloured frontispiece by Norman Wilkinson. J.M. Barrie wrote Barker a number of letters while he was in New York; helpful letters which show what a good friend Barrie was to both parties in the marital trouble.

Later in 1916 Barker returned to England and enlisted in the Royal Horse Artillery; he hated life in the ranks and was admitted to the R.G.A. Cadet School at Trowbridge. Edward Thomas commented ironically on his appearance there, prophesying accurately that Barker's friends in high places would ensure that H.G.B. had a comfortable war. In fact Barker had completed only part of his cadet training when he was given a commission in the General list for special duties in Intelligence.

Though Lillah was convinced for a while that their marriage difficulties would be resolved, in April 1917 she petitioned for divorce; Barker covenanted to pay her £600 a year for life, a sum subsequently increased to £650. Lillah sold the lease of their country house later that year. She and Barker never met again or had any direct communication. Barker's army Intelligence commission did not prevent him from returning to America. Helen Huntington was divorced in 1918 and her husband generously settled a fortune on her. On 31 July 1918 she and H.G.B. were married. Henceforth his wife's considerable wealth would mean that H.G.B. was set free to do what work pleased him most: he chose to write and to continue his studies of Shakespeare, but largely turned his back on the theatre. This pleased Helen who was reluctant for him to mix with his old friends.

In the spring of 1920 Harley and Helen moved into a 17th century house called Netherton Hall, near Honiton in the valley of the River Axe. There they lived a life of some splendour, with liveried servants. Their car was often sent over to Dorchester to transport Thomas Hardy to Netherton, and George Moore stayed for some weekends with them. H.G.B. did a lot of translating and worked on *The Exemplary Theatre*, which he regarded as an important book; it dealt with the function of the theatre and its place in society. A set of proofs of the book was sent to Max Beerbohm who responded by producing five amusing cartoons illustrating 'The theatre of the future.'

In his book *Conversations in Ebury Street* (1924) George Moore devoted one chapter to conversations with H.G.B., termed 'a man of the eighteenth century' by Moore. In it there are references to Barker's book *The Exemplary Theatre* and his play *The Secret Life*. Barker had been at work on this play since 1919; it was completed in 1922 and published the following year. It is about a politician, Evan Stroude, who leaves Britain during a general election in order to see a young woman in America. Barker said of Shakespeare, of whom he was a life-long student, that he was 'searching for some more universal truth which lies behind the ever-shifting appearances of things, some key to their meaning . . . .' In *The Secret Life* Barker appears to be trying to do this himself. Both the characters Oliver and Stroude are obsessed by a Pascalian world-contempt and their insight into 'the misery of man without God.'

> Oliver: "Nothing's much easier, is it, than to make that sort of success if you've the appetite for it . . . . But Evan set out to get past all the tricks, to the heart of things . . . . Is it a stone-dead heart of things, and dare no one say so when he finds out?"

Barker's final play, titled *His Majesty*, was started in 1923 and finished five years later. The play concerns a King who abdicates in a revolutionary situation for personal rather than political reasons. It is an interesting work but has a rather perfunctory ending as if the author had tired of it. The play was not produced though at one time C.B. Cochran considered doing it. Margery Morgan devotes a fifty-page chapter to it, under the title 'Arms and the Man I Sing.'

The Barkers spent a good deal of time travelling, usually staying at the best hotels. Lady Cynthia Asquith, in her book *Portrait of Barrie*, wrote: 'Granville Barker has not—as I'd heard said that he had—lost his charm and personality—how could he—but he does strike me as the worse for wealth. A certain sleeking of the spirit and mind, as well as of body doesn't become him. He looks less like a poet and not wholly unlike a butler. According to Barrie and Elizabeth Lucas (who had just "decorated" his house) his daily life is over-organized by his wife, Helen. The notice "WORKING HOURS NINE UNTIL ONE" hangs on the door of his writing-room . . . . Barrie tells me that Helen is determined not to let him have anything to do with the theatre . . . .'

The organized regime of writing certainly achieved results, for Barker produced a dozen volumes of translations from the Spanish in collaboration with Helen, and several books and pamphlets of lectures, as well as more than a dozen Prefaces to Shakespeare.

In 1930 the Barkers were in Paris looking for another home, and they took a spacious apartment at 18 Place des États-Unis, on the corner of the rue Galilee. They had a staff of eleven, including a Swiss major-domo! During that year Barker gave the Clark Lectures at Trinity College, Cambridge—the lectures were published in the following year with the title *On Dramatic Method*. He spent much of his time studying and writing about Shakespeare; he became President of the Shakespeare Association, succeeding Sir Israel Gollancz, and helped plan and produce the book *A Companion to Shakespeare Studies*.

Harley and Helen also had a busy social life, and they acquired a French country house, the Château de Gregy. In 1937 he was appointed Director of the British Institute in Paris, but resigned from this position at Easter in 1939 because of illness.

In the spring of 1940 Barker was invited to direct a production of *King Lear* at the Old Vic with John Gielgud in the name role. He did this on the understanding that his name would not be used in connection with the production but in fact it was printed on the programme as joint producer with Lewis Casson. After returning to Paris he wrote Gielgud several long letters about the play.

Harley and Helen left Paris at the time of the German invasion in the summer of 1940, leaving their apartment in the hands of an American lawyer. They stayed for a while in Portugal, then sailed to America on 6 September 1940. On arriving in New York they moved into the Mayfair House hotel on Park Avenue. While in America Barker continued to write and lecture, and a two-volume edition of his *Prefaces to Shakespeare* was published by the Princeton University Press in 1946.

After going back to England in 1945 the Barkers returned to Paris in the spring of 1946. They found that their apartment was still in good state, but H.G.B. was troubled by illness. When he was asked to broadcast for

Shaw's ninetieth birthday he replied, 'Thank you, but it must, I fear, definitely be "No." A stupid little illness prevents me doing any immediate work . . . .' Soon after this he had a fall in which he broke two ribs. Subsequently he was ill with pneumonia and then had a violent cardiac attack. He was also depressed and suffering from delusions; he said to a friend 'I feel my life is useless.'

He died, at the age of sixty-eight, on 31 August 1946; the cause of death was arterio-sclerosis. His body was embalmed and buried in the cemetery called Pére Lachaise, where Oscar Wilde is buried. The stone was engraved only with his name and dates. After his death G.B. Shaw protested that the obituaries had not said enough about his work as a playwright and commented: ' . . . his original contributions to our dramatic literature are treasures to be preserved.'

* * * * * * * * * *

I included a large batch of Granville Barker items from Lady Keeble's collection in my catalogue 51, issued in September 1961, stressing the fact that most of Barker's major manuscripts were in the British Museum, having been purchased from the Institut Britannique in Paris, and so would never come on the market. Among the original letters was an early one written by Barker to his mother on 1 August 1895; this was sent from Guernsey while he was on tour with Ben Greet's theatrical company, and was signed 'Little Boy'. A more important letter was a signed draft of one sent to Herbert Samuel on 24 May 1909 about censorship: ' . . . As I read through my report of my evidence it seems that I did not make at all clear my views as to the control of the Theatre alternative to that of the Lord Chamberlain . . . .' There were also some cards that Barker had addressed to Lillah in 1912 while he was on holiday in the Pyrenees: 'This is the haunted & stricken valley where we camped for 24 hours in the rain in a thing like a crowded railway carriage made of jagged rock under a leaky tent without poles, without firewood & not enough to eat . . . .'

There were several typescripts of plays, much annotated by Barker and various authors, and the manuscript of an unpublished play by Lillah McCarthy dated December 1915 and titled 'Progress'. With this MS there was also a note by Margery Morgan about the play: ' . . . the character of Matthew Brodie is undoubtedly a portrait of Granville Barker as his wife saw him at the time of the break-up of their marriage . . . .' A copy of Thomas Hardy's book *Time's Laughingstocks and other Verses* was inscribed to Lillah

65

by Hardy and heavily annotated by her because she gave public recitals of some of the poems.

The most interesting Barker item in my catalogue 54 (Autumn 1962) was a copy of Hardy's *The Dynasts*, 1910, a good deal cut and annotated by H.G.B. On page 512 he had written: 'Here I badly want a vivid and dramatic stage direction bridging from p. 507 to this moment, the climax of the battle. And to emphasise the climax a lyrical chorus would be invaluable. Perhaps we can't do better than the Chorus of Rumours (p. 512) but we might. And the whole act (as the battle) hinges on this moment . . . .' The book was also inscribed and annotated by Lillah.

In catalogue 55, 'The Edwardians', I listed an original drawing of Barker by Max Beerbohm showing H.G.B. standing at his bookshelves (a variant of this drawing was used for his bookplate); this was signed, titled and dated 1907. In the same catalogue there was a copy of Barker's *A Companion to Shakespeare Studies*, 1934, inscribed by the author to the Beerbohms; loosely inserted in this there was a sketch by Max of H.G.B.

By far the most important and interesting Granville Barker material was described in catalogue 63 (Spring 1966). Some of it came from Lillah's collection but other items I had bought at Sotheby's and these, apparently, emanated from C.B. Purdom's archive. Item 16 was of the typescript notes made by Arnold Bennett for Lillah's use in his play *Judith* (1919). Bennett had written in his *Journals* comments about Harley & Lillah when they were staying together at the Royal York Hotel in Brighton in 1910: 'Granville Barker . . . . Very intelligent and nice . . . . No worldly conversation. I mean no polite, insincere interest shown in personal things that come up . . . . Wife the same. She is a different woman when animated and fifty times better . . . .' In his *Journal* for 1919 Bennett tells how he came to write *Judith* for Lillah and gives an account of early performances of the play: 'I never took so much interest in the production of a play of mine . . . . (Lillah) her tent costume frightened one of the lessees of the theatre. Above a line drawn about 1/2 inch or 1 inch above the "mont de Venus" she wore nothing except a 4-in. band of black velvet round the body hiding the breasts and going down to the skirt and so hiding the navel . . . . She looked a magnificent picture thus . . . .'

Item 87 was a Barker original manuscript, probably the only one ever offered for sale in this country: the MS of his unfinished and unpublished play *The Wicked Man*. Margery Morgan gave an account of it in her book: 'There survives among Barker's manuscripts a fragmentary record of the actual process of composing a long play. This includes, among other notes, three versions of the opening of a play to be called The Village Carpenter, together with two versions of the beginning of Act III . . . . The notes for The Village Carpenter, of which there are thirty large sheets, seem to have been made in 1910; for among them appear a few notes for an article on Barrie, which was published in *The Bookman* that year. The scraps towards The Wicked Man are on notepaper with printed headings: "17 John Street, Adelphi" whither the Barkers moved early in 1911, and "Kingsway Theatre" the lease of which was taken at the end of 1911, as well as "Court Lodge, Stansted" where he was known to be writing in 1911. Certain of the *dramatis personae* of The Village Carpenter appear in two Acts of The Wicked Man and, despite considerable differences between them, the two plays reveal themselves, upon closer study, to be one. By a process of continual revision and re-thinking, The Wicked Man grew out of the earlier attempt . . . . A fact immediately apparent is that Barker's thoughts had gone back to his earliest published play; for first in the list of characters under the title, The Village Carpenter, is the name "John Baptist Abud", and John Abud is retained among the chief characters in The Wicked Man. A disconnected note identifies him as the grandson of the earlier Abud, the youngest descendant of the large family come of Ann Leete's union with the gardener . . . . The original title and the names, Elisabeth, Mary, John Baptist Abud, suggest that Barker had Christian, messianic symbolism in mind . . . .'

The next item consisted of the original, heavily corrected typescripts of two versions of the play *The Weather-Hen* written by Barker in collaboration with Berte Thomas. Margery Morgan had commented on this: ' . . . Although Berte Thomas was nine years older than Barker, the dominant personality . . . is certainly the younger man's . . . . Thomas has stated that his own part in the work was increasingly that of a secretary and that, as he wrote down the dialogue of Our Visitor, he understood hardly a word of it. . . .'

Another important item consisted of Barker's love letters to Helen Huntington, a series of sixty on over 300 4to pages. These were of an intimate nature so I did not quote from them but recorded Purdom's comments on the relationship and those made by Margery Morgan: 'The later story, *Souls on Fifth*, bears marks of being a love-gift for Helen Huntington. It seems to have been written late in 1915 or early in 1916, during the time of waiting for his divorce . . . . The author seems to be playing with the facts of a personal situation for an intimate, sympathetic eye . . . . The author's sense of life is most convincingly present in the evocation of loneliness . . . .'

A group of Barker's passports, visa applications and correspondence included an interesting letter from their American lawyer, Pendleton Beckley, who looked after their Paris flat during the war: 'In August 1942 I was arrested by the Gestapo . . . . My wife was questioned at Gestapo headquarters, 31 bis Avenue Foch, by Lt. Meindle of the German police . . . . At that moment my wife burnt all the visiting cards belonging to the Granville Barkers as they had been visited by many people who might have been in difficulty to explain in case of investigation . . . .'

Item 103 consisted of a group of letters written by Helen to Harley during the 1939-45 War when they were temporarily parted: some from their French apartment when Harley was in London, and others from Mayfair House, New York, when he was at Harvard. ' . . . I wish Harvard had the despicable comforts of Mayfair House for you—and remember the verses about the sandpiper "My driftwood fire will burn so bright—To what warm shelter can'st *thou* fly?"; Forgive me—and don't be cross—if I don't send my book. I've just read it over and I do feel the thing most to be desired for it—by us both—is oblivion. I did have a poetic impulse—and perhaps some poetic feeling—nothing more . . . .'

Two proof copies, bound together, of Lillah's autobiography, *Myself and my friends*, published in 1933, were also included. The first proof varied a good deal from the published text: for example, pp. 188/9 which began, 'It brought me no comfort then. I wanted pity and I got advice. But Shaw knows the art of giving something better in place of that for which the downcast crave . . . .' were deleted. Purdom gave an account of this book's chequered career; the difficulties arose when Barker was sent a proof copy: 'Barker made it clear that there should be no reference whatever to himself anywhere in the book. With every mention of Barker, direct or indirect, eliminated, Lillah thought the book should not be published, and would have no more to do with it; but her husband did not agree and took over the book to re-write it, which he did thoroughly . . . .' Sir Frederick Keeble may well have master-minded the revision of the book but there was no doubt that many of the corrections were in Lillah's hand.

There was a rough proof of Shaw's *Pygmalion*, 1913 with stage directions written in pencil. Shaw at first contemplated putting on *Pygmalion* with Barker, as is shown in *The Shaw-Barker Letters* (1956): ' . . . I want to know before I move again in the matter of Pygmalion. I really don't see why Pygmalion should go out of the family.' But, as Purdom noted, 'Pygmalion was not done until Beerbohm Tree put it on at His Majesty's Theatre on 11 April 1914 . . . .'

The auctioneers nodded over one item from the Purdom collection and I displayed some glee in demonstrating this. It was a small thing, but it seemed to me of significance in the story of Harley Granville Barker, echoing the 'Rosebud' theme in Orson Welles' cinematic masterpiece *Citizen Kane*. I am reproducing my catalogue description word for word:

MINIATURE OF HIS MOTHER AT THE AGE OF NINETEEN. A highly finished and charming little painting of Mary Elisabeth Bozzi-Granville in an oval silver locket with a lock of her hair preserved under a glass at the back, engraved: "M.E.B.G. June 1st, 1868." Barker's mother was the daughter of Augustus Bozzi; she was born in 1849; "She was something of a success on the public platform in this country and America when poetry recitals were a regular form of cultural entertainment. Harley took after his mother in appearance. Indeed there was a marked Granville family likeness in the shape of his head and his complexion . . .. In the spring of 1891, at the age of thirteen, he was with his mother at Harrogate and made his first public appearance in a play . . .." This locket was included in a miscellaneous lot by Sotheby's and not described by them; the silver was dirty and the glass so obscured that it was impossible to say whose portrait it covered, but we felt that it must have been of some importance to Barker for him to have preserved it through all his many moves and the various vicissitudes of his life. We cleaned it and behold: "Rosebud"!

7. — *BREDE PLACE & 'THE GHOST'*

In the summer of 1897 when Stephen Crane, the author of *The Red Badge of Courage*, was twenty-six he was living with his 'wife' Cora in a house in Oxted, Surrey, called 'Ravensbrook Villa'. At that time the Cranes contributed a Sunday newsletter, under the pseudonym 'Imogene Carter', which was published in the *New York Press*, and one of their articles commented: 'Life in an English country house is perhaps the most delightful manner of living in the world, and society must be forgiven if it grows silly over it . . . .' Though he was unusually adventurous for an author, and very much a wanderer, it is clear that such a mode of living did appeal to Stephen Crane.

The mysterious sinking of the battleship 'Maine' in 1898 led to war between the U.S.A. and Cuba. At the height of the newspaper campaign conducted by the American press for an invasion of Cuba, Henry James's reactions to the affair were set out in a letter he wrote to his brother: 'I confess that the blaze about to come leaves me awfully cold, thrilling with no glorious thrill or holy blood-thirst whatever. I see nothing but madness, the passion, the hideous clumsiness of rage, of mechanical reverberation; and I echo with all my heart your denouncement of the screeching newspaper.' The reaction to the war of James's young friend Stephen Crane was quite different; he was hard-up and welcomed the opportunity to do some war reporting. Another of Crane's friends, Joseph Conrad, later recalled that one April afternoon in 1898 Crane had come to him to seek help in obtaining sixty pounds with which to get to Cuba, ' . . . before the sun set, before dinner, before the "six-forty" train to Oxted, at once, that instant—lest peace should be declared and the opportunity of seeing a war be missed. I had not sixty pounds to lend him. Sixty shillings was nearer my mark . . . . Crane's white-faced excitement frightened me. Finally it occurred to me to take him to Messrs. Blackwood & Sons' London office. There he was received in a most friendly way. Presently I escorted him to Charing Cross, where he took the train for home with the assurance that he would have the means to start "for the war" next day.' To obtain the money it was necessary for Conrad to mortgage his own future literary earnings as security for fifty pounds, while Sanford Bennett provided an additional ten pounds.

Crane had an adventurous time for the rest of 1898, accompanying American soldiers in the jungles and on the beaches. When the Americans invaded Puerto Rico Crane was there, and indeed he was the first American to enter the town of Juana Diaz. His friend Richard Harding Davis reported that 'The *alcalde* had surrendered the town to its lone invader . . . . Crane told me that no general in the moment of victory had ever acted in a more generous manner. He shot no one against a wall, looted no churches, levied no forced loans. Instead he lined up the male members of the community in the plaza, and organized a joint celebration of the conquerors and conquered . . . that overflowed from the plaza into the by-streets and lashed itself into a frenzied carnival of rejoicing . . . .'

When Stephen Crane was in Cuba, Cora in Oxted was being besieged by creditors. As she was not legally married to Crane, Cora was anxious in case this fact should leak out and she should find herself liable for all the debts. She desperately appealed to Crane's friends for help and one of them, Moreton Frewen, offered to lend the couple a country estate he owned called Brede Place a few miles west of Rye. Crane returned to England on the steamer 'Manitou' which reached Gravesend on January 11, 1899. On the 13th January Crane sent Conrad a telegraph order for fifty guineas, and repaid Sanford Bennett the ten pounds.

Immediately he saw Brede Place, Stephen Crane felt much happier and more confident about the future. The Cranes drove to the manor house from the railway station at Hastings and improvised a supper of ham and eggs from provisions in a hamper. Cora wrote to Edward Garnett: 'We are going to move Heaven and Earth to get there. Stephen said that a solemn feeling of work came to him there; so I am delighted.' Garnett commented: 'It was the lure of romance that always thrilled Crane's blood, and Brede Place had had indeed, an unlucky, chequered history.' The oldest wing of the house had been built in 1378. In 1899 it stood gaunt and empty, its windows black and broken, the grounds like a jungle. There were no bathrooms, lavatories or running water; no lighting apart from candles. Despite these drawbacks the Cranes were thrilled at the prospect of living there and they moved in on Sunday the 12th February.

The first room that the Cranes put into order was a study in the cubicle over the porch so that Stephen could start churning out articles and stories. R.W. Stallman, Crane's biographer, wrote of this time: 'He was writing against the clock, without time to let themes ripen in his mind, and he could not afford to tear up a first draft or start on a better line. To obtain advances from Pinker he was writing things that came easily to him . . . .'

Ford Madox Ford wrote: 'I formed a very disagreeable impression of Brede. It seemed to be full of evil influences, to be very damp, and to be hopelessly remote . . . with its deep hollows, dank coppices, and precipitous hop-fields . . . full of hobgoblins and miasmas . . . .' But Stephen Crane took a different view and wrote to Mrs. Frewen that whatever happened at Brede they found it 'delightful': 'During these late heavy storms the whole house sang like a harp and all the spooks have been wailing to us. It is rather valkyric. The servants are more impressed than we would like them to be and we have not yet found maids who will sleep in the house . . . .' To Moreton Frewen Crane wrote: 'If you can stay the night we will be very glad and can put you up comfortably. The ghost has been walking lately but we cannot catch him. Perhaps when the real Frewen sleeps under his roof he may condescend to display himself to all of us.'

Though Crane joked about the sensation of the house being haunted it was a serious factor in living at Brede Place and remained so for many years. In 1899 the house was like a draughty shell of a place with many rooms unfurnished and unlit even by flickering candles. The novelist A.E.W. Mason wrote about sleeping in a room at one end of which were double doors which he opened after dark and ' . . . found that if I had taken one step forward I should have stepped down about thirty feet into the chapel, this room being the private pew or box of the owners of the house . . . .' Bats flew about Mason's room until he snuffed out his candle when they settled down to share the room with him. It is not surprising that he slept badly.

Stephen Crane put Brede into his story 'The Squire's Madness' and his novel *The O'Ruddy* in which Sir Goddard Oxenbridge's altar tomb is in Brede Church. Mark Barr, transported to Brede from Rye railway station in a wagonette drawn by hay horses named Hengist and Horsa, was informed that the ghost often visited a circular room in the tower; footsteps would be heard there and the door of the room would open mysteriously. Edith Ritchie, Crane's niece, recalled staying at Brede Place in June, 1899: 'Outside my windows was thick ivy in which white owls roosted, and their hoo-hoo-hoos were eerie if you didn't know where they came from. The room had three doors, leading to other rooms or halls. When I went up to dress for dinner, I would carefully close each door. A moment later I would look fearsomely over my left shoulder. Door number one would be open. Then, over my right shoulder, door number two open, and, a little further to the right, door number three. I always turned slowly and always had the same spooky feeling . . . .'

Later that year Crane used the theme of a ghost for a short play, which he looked on purely as light entertainment and did not take seriously. He then had the idea of making it sound more interesting, which he outlined in a letter to H.B. Marriott Watson: 'We of Brede Place are giving a free play to the villagers at Christmas time in the school-house and I have written some awful rubbish which our friends will on that night speak out to the parish. But to make the thing historic, I have hit on the plan of making the programmes choice by printing thereon a terrible list of authors of the comedy and to that end I have asked Henry James, Robert Barr, Joseph Conrad, A.E.W. Mason, H.G. Wells, Edwin Pugh, George Gissing, Rider Haggard and yourself to write a mere word—any word, "it", "they", "you", any word and thus identify themselves in this crime. Would you be so lenient as to give me the word in your hand writing and thus appear in print on the programme with this distinguished rabble?'

In his book *Authors and I*, Charles Hind wrote: 'I received an invitation to spend three days in Brede Place, on the second day a play was to be performed in the schoolroom in Brede village, a mile away up the hill. This play we were informed, sub rosa, had been written by Henry James, H.G. Wells, A.E.W. Mason and other lights of literature. Duly I arrived at Brede Place. Surely there has never been such a house party. The ancient house, in spite of its size, was taxed to the uppermost. There were six men in the vast, bare chamber where I slept; the six iron bedsteads, procured for the occasion, quite lost in the amplitude of the chamber . . .. Of the play I have no recollection. The performance has been driven from my mind by the memory of the agony of getting to Brede village. It was a pouring wet night, with thunder and lightning. The omnibuses which transported us up the hill stuck in the miry roads. Again and again we had to alight and push, and each time we returned to our seats on top I remarked to my neighbour, H. G. Wells, that Brede village is not a suitable place for dramatic performances.'

The play was performed at 7.45 p.m. on December 28. A.E.W. Mason was the only celebrity to act, taking the part of 'the Ghost': Mrs. H.G.

Wells played the piano to accompany such songs as 'Three Little Maids of Rye.' No London critic saw the play but a review appeared in the *Sussex Express*, identifying the performers as 'the Brede Place house party, assisted by a few friends' and noting that 'Mr. Stephen Crane paid all the expenses in producing the play.' In the biography of A.E.W. Mason the play was called 'a literary *jeu d'esprit* perhaps made more intriguing from the fact that after its production the only copy was destroyed, and even the cast was not allowed to be published.' In fact the cast was printed in a programme of which at least one copy has survived—now in the Berg Collection at the New York Public Library.

After the performance there was a party at Brede Place which went on into the early hours, with dancing in a hall lit by large candles burning in sconces improvised by the local blacksmith. The guests then slept until noon when they breakfasted on bacon and eggs, American sweet potatoes and beer. Afterwards Crane persuaded his guests to learn American-style poker, which none of them took seriously, chattering all the time. He complained, 'In any decent saloon in America you'd be shot for talking like that at poker.'

H.G. Wells thought this was a 'sulky reaction.' He wrote that Crane '. . . was profoundly weary and ill, if I had been wise enough to see it . . . . He was essentially the helpless artist; he wasn't master of his party; he wasn't master of his home; his life was altogether out of control . . . . Sensation and expression—and with him it had been well nigh perfect expression—was the supreme joy of his life and the justification of existence for him. And here he was, in a medley of impulsive disproportionate expenditure, being pursued by the worthy Pinker with enquiries of when he could "deliver copy" . . . .'

Soon after most of his guests had departed Stephen Crane collapsed, and H.G. Wells set off on a bicycle to Rye to fetch a doctor. Crane appeared to recover quickly and on New Year's Eve he toasted a friend, saying: 'Let us drink to the twentieth century—in spite of your objection, Mark.' This was because Mark Barr had insisted that 1900 was the last year of the nineteenth century, not the first year of the new one.

After his apparent recovery Crane worked steadily on his novel, *The O'Ruddy*, and by February had completed nearly forty thousand words of it. In March one day his mouth filled with blood and Cora spent fifty pounds in sending for a London physician. In writing to Pinker for the money she added, 'If Mr. Crane should die I have notes of the end of the novel so it could be finished & no one will lose . . . .'

Friends considered that Cora's behaviour, including the spending of much-needed money on some restoration work at Brede Place, was eccentric, and similarly erratic behaviour is to be seen in the last story Crane worked on, 'The Squire's Madness.' The squire is not sure whether he or his wife is mentally ill, and a London brain specialist tells him, 'It is your wife who is mad! Mad as a hatter!'

Ford Madox Ford wrote that Henry James was particularly concerned about the dying young man, and it is said that James's novel *The Sacred Fount* owes something of its poignancy to the Crane affair. Leon Edel wrote of ' . . . the vision the novelist had of the way in which Crane was visibly dying while Cora thrived, seemingly unaware of the tragedy being lived under her roof. It was an old theme with James—the way in which men and women prey on one another.'

When Cora decided they should go to Badenweiler in the Black Forest James sent her fifty pounds, asking her to 'dedicate it to whatever service might best render my stricken friend. It meagrely represents my tender benediction to him.'

Moreton Frewen and other friends also gave Cora some money and the Cranes took the channel steamer from Dover. Conrad came to see them at the Lord Warden Hotel near the Admiralty pier. Wells visited them too, and wrote of Crane 'lying still and comfortably wrapped about before an open window and the calm and spacious sea. If you would figure him as I saw him, you must think of him as a face of a type very typically American, long and spare, with very straight features and long, quiet hands and hollow eyes, moving very slowly, smiling and speaking slowly, with that deliberate New Jersey manner he had, and lapsing from speech again into a quiet contemplation of his ancient enemy . . . .'

In Badenweiler Crane finally titled the novel *The O'Ruddy*, and whispered suggestions about its conclusion. Cora wrote to Moreton Frewen: 'He lives over everything in dreams and talks aloud constantly . . . .' Stephen Crane died at 3 a.m. on June 5, 1900. Moreton Frewen, the real squire of Brede Place, took the news to Henry James at Lamb House, Rye. James wrote to Cora: 'What a brutal needless extinction—what an unmitigated, unredeemed catastrophe! I think of him with such a sense of possibilities & powers! . . . Shall you come back—for any time at all—to Brede Place? You will of course hate to—but it occurs to me that you may have things to do there, or possessions to collect . . . .' Cora took Crane's body on the *Bremen* to New York. A little later in the summer a van removed the Cranes' few possessions from Brede Place.

8. ——— *OSCAR WILDE'S LAST DAYS*

At the outset of my book-dealing career I had a great stroke of luck. In the summer of 1948 I wrote to Julian Symons, brother of the author of *The Quest for Corvo*, asking him if any proof sections existed of A.J.A. Symons' mammoth unpublished bibliography of 1890s authors. In reply I had a friendly letter from Julian, written from his flat in Blackheath, inviting me to call there and see the surviving proofs. From our first meeting we got on well and over the next few months I made a number of other visits to Blackheath, and then to the Symons' family home in Clapham, a house called 'Mount Lebanon', where I bought many books and other literary material left by A.J.A.

Items from his collection added a good deal of interest to my second catalogue (issued in the winter of 1948) and included letters from 'Baron Corvo' (Frederick Rolfe), Olive Custance (the poetess who married Lord Alfred Douglas), Eric Gill, John Gray, Vincent O'Sullivan, Robert H. Sherard (an early biographer of Oscar Wilde), John Addington Symonds, and Thomas J. Wise. A notable letter also listed was one written by Ernest Dowson to his friend Charles Sayle, setting forth his attitude to life and art: 'I exist, you perceive, and much more than that I have never done . . . . I have a Sonnet in this month's 'Temple Bar', that is all and that is nothing for I have never done more than play with verse . . . . But beyond anything I envy you your Catholicism . . . but one is not with impunity of this damned, fastidious, fascinating century . . . . And sooner or later to anything in life and art, the cursed critical devil pops up with his "Cui bono?" And I, for one, can not answer him.'

As a kind of postscript to my Catalogue 2 I described the large collection of letters written by Lord Alfred Douglas to A.J.A. Symons from 1928 to

1941. There were 130 letters and most of them dealt with literary matters; I said that the collection 'contains unpublished material of considerable importance.' There was much about Wilde in this correspondence: 'On mature consideration I now feel certain that it must have been 1891 when I first met O.W. . . . also as the first night of Lady Windermere's Fan was in Feb. 1892 that is additional evidence as by that time I had known him for a few months . . . . I wrote an appreciation of Salomé in May, 1893 and it was a result of this appreciation that Oscar asked me to translate it. I did so in the summer vacation of 1893 . . . .'

Before his premature death in 1941 A.J.A. Symons had been preparing a biography of Oscar Wilde. He had written three chapters of it, two of which were published in *Horizon*. Julian Symons later wrote about this projected book: ' . . . One other completed chapter, on Wilde's attempt to conquer Paris, has been lost. Enough remains, I think, to show that the book would really have been a study that made others unnecessary and that it might have been one of the high points of English biography.' A.J.A. began to collect material concerning Wilde in the 1920s when it was still possible to meet a number of people like Douglas who had known O.W.; with others, such as Vincent O'Sullivan, scattered about the world, he conducted long correspondences. A.J.A. was also a close friend of Christopher Millard, author under the pen-name 'Stuart Mason' of the exhaustive Wilde bibliography, and that was a great help in his quest. It was from Millard that A.J.A. purchased many items which had come from Robert Ross.

I was fortunate enough to dispose of most of this Wilde material, largely through catalogues I issued from 1948 to 1950. A number of the most interesting letters were listed in my third catalogue (Spring, 1949). Among them were four letters written by Reginald Turner to Robert Ross during the last week of Wilde's illness. The first letter was dated Monday (26 November 1900): 'I had today a long talk with the patron of the Hotel d'Alsace. At the consultation yesterday the doctors gave very little hope of Oscar's recovery, and Tucker was very anxious that you should be sent for . . . the patron wants you to write to him as to anyone who should be sent for in the case of Oscar getting worse . . . . As to Oscar, he of course knows nothing of what they say, he is beyond taking notice, his mind wanders and he sleeps. That is I think partly the result of the morphine which they inject into him, but now that is forbidden, so they are only going to pretend to inject . . . .' The second letter was dated 27 November: 'Please send directions at once as to who is to be communicated with if Oscar dies . . . . I am rather muddled. Tucker wired me to warn Oscar's family and on my going to see him (Tucker) he told me Oscar might die at any minute and that his mind was gone. On coming here I found Oscar better, the mind clear and able to talk, but his utterance is thick and his eyes odd . . . . If Oscar dies, Harris must hand over the money to you or some responsible person who will pay the debts to these people who have been so good to Oscar. He is very difficult, makes scenes and refuses to allow them to put mustard plasters on his legs. His head is kept in ice. He takes hardly any nourishment . . . .'

The fourth letter was also dated Wednesday, having been sent off in the evening. ' . . . Just now Oscar seems a little easier. After holding an ice bag on his head for three-quarters of an hour he said to me, "You dear little Jew, don't you think that's enough?" He talked to you about his play today, said it was worth fifty centimes . . . .'

There was a postscript, dated 6 p.m., to this final letter: ' . . . Oscar is a little better, but Tucker cannot say it means anything . . . . Tucker and the specialist made me and the patron sign a paper giving an account of the consultation so that his sons may see if they want to at any future time that all possible is being done for him . . . .'

Another letter of comparable interest in the same catalogue was one I sold to Mr. H. Montgomery Hyde. This was written on sixteen pages by Robert Ross and addressed to Adela Schuster on 23 December 1900, from the Hôtel Belle Vue, Mentone: ' . . . About five days before I left for Nice he caught a slight cold in the ear and this developed into an abcess, rapidly, *causing him great pain*. No importance was attached to it by the English doctor, but the French doctor regarded it as a grave symptom. It was much better on November 13th. It was, however, the abcess which eventually produced inflammation of the brain . . . . On Sunday the 25th he did not get up, complained of giddiness and during the evening became light-headed . . . . He was never able to *articulate* after my arrival. It was most fortunate that Mr. Turner, whom he knew very well, was with him the whole of the last week of his life. Till Sunday 25th he was able to laugh and talk, though he got easily tired and he believed he was dying. I am thankful I arrived in time, as there was no other person there who could assume any authority or knew of his affairs . . . . Two things were absolutely necessary to him, contact with comely things, as Pater says, and social position. Comely things meant for him a certain standard of living, and this, since his release, he *was able to have* except for a few weeks at a time, or perhaps months. Social position he realized after five months he could not have . . . . I was not surprised by the silence of the press. Journalists could hardly say very much, and it was better to be silent than point a moral. Later on I think everyone will recognize his achievements; his plays and essays will endure . . . . Some time I should be very grateful if you allowed me to have your views as to the advisability of a memoir, and its scope or plan, and if done with discretion whether it would please and interest his friends. I would not care for it to appeal to morbid curiosity, and I remember Mr. Wilde's remark "that it is always Judas who writes the biography" . . . .'

Cataloguing this rich material made me become very interested in the last period of Wilde's life and I read everything I could find about it. This, of course, was years before the three editions of his Letters, splendidly edited by Sir Rupert Hart-Davis. Nevertheless I managed to read many of them in catalogues such as the fine one produced by Dulau, and the various biographical works then available including Frank Harris's *Oscar Wilde, His Life and Confessions* (New York, 1918). The overwhelming impression I had from Wilde's letters was of his courage in adversity and what has been called 'his indestructible gaiety.' For example see the letter he wrote to his devious publisher Leonard Smithers on 9 May 1898 (this a day after he had written to Robert Ross that 'I had not a penny, and had to stay in my room, and as they only give breakfast at the hotel, I was dinnerless.'): 'You are so accustomed to bringing out books limited to three copies, one for the author, one for yourself, and one for the Police, that I really believe you are sinking beneath your standard in producing a sixpenny edition of anything. Perhaps as I want the poem to reach the poorer classes, we might give away a cake of Maypole soap with each copy: I hear it dyes people the most lovely colours. . . .'

An early sign of illness in the final year was a complaint in a letter to Robert Ross in February: 'Paris is awful. I have also been poisoned by mussels—a dreadful thing.' In a letter postmarked 22 October 1900 Wilde wrote to Frank Harris about an operation he had arranged in the expectation of receiving £175 from the egregious Frank: ' . . . Fully believing in you I arranged to be operated on by one of the first surgeons of Paris: the operation took place ten days ago under chloroform. I was obliged to draw post-dated cheques for the fees, which were enormous. I have also been obliged to have a *garde-malade*, and a doctor to sleep in the same room at night, besides a consulting physician. My debts and expenses are appalling—not less than £150. I relied on your honour to carry out your agreement . . . .'

It seems that Maurice a'Court Tucker, the British Embassy doctor who attended Wilde, at first misunderstood his case though Tucker was attentive enough, paying his patient some sixty-eight visits, commencing on 27

September. He and Dr. Paul Cleiss held a consultation on 27 November and issued a report saying they had ' . . . established that there were significant cerebral disturbances stemming from an old suppuration of the right ear, under treatment for several years. On the 27th, the symptoms became much graver. The diagnosis of encephalitic meningitis must be made without doubt. In the absence of any indication of localization, trepanning cannot be contemplated . . . .' Modern medical opinion is that Wilde died of an intercranial complication of suppurative *otis media*, or middle-ear disease.

When Wilde was known to be dying Robert Ross went to the Passionist Fathers and brought Father Cuthbert Dunne to the bedside. 'At 5.30 a.m., to the consternation of Ross and Turner, a loud, strong death rattle began, like the turning of a crank. Foam and blood came from his mouth during the morning, and at ten minutes to two in the afternoon Wilde died. (The death certificate says the time was 2 p.m. on 30 November.)'

On 14 December 1900 Ross wrote to More Adey, another of Wilde's close friends, giving some rather distressing details of the death and subsequent events: ' . . . It was in the afternoon the District Doctor called and asked if Oscar had committed suicide or was murdered. He would not look at the signed certificates of Klein and Tucker. Gesling had warned me the previous evening that owing to the assumed name and Oscar's identity, the authorities might insist on his body being taken to the Morgue. Of course I was appalled at the prospect; it really seemed the final touch of horror. After examining the body, and, indeed, everybody in the hotel, and after a series of drinks and unseasonable jests, and a liberal fee, the District Doctor consented to sign the permission for burial. Then arrived some other revolting official; he asked how many collars Oscar had, and the value of his umbrella, (this is quite true, and not a mere exaggeration of mine.) Then various poets and literary people called, Raymond de la Tailhade, Tardieu, Charles Sibleigh, Jehan Rictus, Robert d'Humieres, George Sinclair, and various English people, who gave assumed names, together with two veiled women. They were all allowed to see the body when they signed their names. . . .'

Wilde's funeral service took place at the Church of St. Germain-des-Prés on 3 December 1900. There were four carriages in the cortège, the first occupied by Lord Alfred Douglas, Robert Ross, Reginald Turner and Jean Dupoirer (the proprietor of the Hôtel d'Alsace who sent a bead trophy, to place on the coffin, inscribed 'A mon locataire'). The body was buried at Bagneux and later a tombstone was set above it, bearing an inscription from the twenty-sixth chapter of the Book of Job.

A succinct comment on Wilde's fate was made by Robert Ross in a letter to Louis Wilkinson: 'He was very unhappy, and would have become more unhappy as time went on.'

In 1909 Wilde's corpse was removed from Bagneux and taken to the Père Lachaise cemetery in Paris where it now rests under a monument sculpted by Jacob Epstein. Eric Gill designed an inscription for the stone which was engraved by his assistant, Joseph Cribb. It ends with an epitaph taken from *The Ballad of Reading Gaol*:

> And alien tears will fill for him
>   Pity's long broken urn.
> For his mourners will be outcast men
>   And outcasts always mourn.

9. —— OLIVER ST. JOHN GOGARTY

I have only been able to build a small pantheon for Heroes. Supreme, mysterious, Shakespeare stands centre stage, flanked by Tolstoy and Dickens. Next to Dickens is the bulky figure of Orson Welles. Orson is there because his cinematic masterpieces *Citizen Kane* and *The Magnificent Ambersons* had a profound, challenging effect on my imagination when I was a young man. I can readily visualize the opening images of Kane with the camera focused on a distant, lit window in the fairy-tale castle called Xanadu before taking in the barbed wire and iron grill work, then travelling up a gateway of seemingly gigantic proportions with the huge initial 'K' growing ever darker against the dawn sky. And I shall never forget certain scenes in Ambersons, such as the one at the dinner table where Eugene Morgan (Joseph Cotten) somewhat reluctantly has to agree with Georgie Amberson Minafer (Tim Holt) that the invention of the automobile might not be an unmixed blessing. Orson is not only a bulky figure on the dais but he tends to move about a bit, muttering 'flawed masterpieces', a criticism which rather irked him at the end of his life. Nevertheless I should like to find room on the platform for Oliver St. John Gogarty. Gogarty was not a genius like Shakespeare, nor did he have an outstanding imaginative gift, but he did have other qualities which I both admire and envy. Truly he was a man for all seasons!

About 1950 I bought a large collection of books by Gogarty from the remarkably fine library of R.N. Greene-Armytage which was housed at No. 5 Queen's Parade in Bath. Most of Gogarty's well-known books—*As I was Going Down Sackville Street* (1937), *Tumbling in the Hay* (1939), *Mr. Petunia* (1945) and *Mourning Became Mrs. Spendlove* (1948)—were there, together with a few rarities like the Cuala Press edition of *Wild Apples* (1930) and *The Ship* (1918). The collection did not include Gogarty's first book, *Hyperthuleana*

(1916), nor have I ever seen a copy. Greene-Armytage was a retired barrister and bibliophile who had collected books all his life. He was a man of great charm with a fund of anecdotes about authors he had known, and others he had admired from afar. Sometimes, when I was trying to concentrate on the books on his shelves, I might grow a trifle impatient as he dilated on the nuances of, say, a letter written by Lord Alfred Douglas in 1910, but I learnt a great deal in listening to him.

It was from Greene-Armytage that I first heard anecdotes of Gogarty, including the one of his escape from assassins, crucial from my point of view. Oh for a quarter of Gogarty's courage and wit! When Gogarty was a Senator in the Irish Free State an attempt was made on his life by anti-Treaty forces: he was ordered into a car at pistol point and driven off to be executed in a house at Islandbridge, on the River Liffey. 'Death by shooting is a very good death,' he was assured. 'When he got out of the car he asked, "Shall I tip the driver?" Later, on the pretext of an urgent call of nature, he asked to be taken outside . . . . "Would you mind holding my coat?" he pleaded in a distressed voice and as the gunmen's attention was distracted by holding the coat he plunged away from them, sprang towards the river bank and dived into the ice-cold Liffey. Shots were fired at him as he swam to freedom.'

Gogarty's escape from his would-be killers and his subsequent arrival, dripping wet, at the local police station were celebrated in a popular ballad which ended:

> Cried Oliver St. John Gogarty, "A Senator am I!
> The rebels I've tricked, the river I've swum
>   and sorra the word's a lie."
> As they clad and fed the hero bold, said the
>   sergeant with a wink:
> "Faith then, Oliver St. John Gogarty, ye've
>   too much bounce to sink."

From the 1950s I always bought books by Gogarty when they came my way, and on a few occasions I talked about him with Harford Montgomery Hyde who had been one of his friends. I included a handful of presentation copies inscribed to Harford in my Catalogue 102, where I also quoted an interesting letter from Gogarty to A.J.A. Symons: 'You were the first one to realise what a dominating influence Mahaffy had on Wilde . . . .'

A little later, in 1979, I was fortunate enough to buy the Gogarty collection of George Redding who had been a close friend of Gogarty from early days. There were some unusually interesting items in this collection

and I included a few of them in my Catalogue 104; this is my description
of one of them:

78 AN OFFERING OF SWANS. *Cuala Press*, 1923. The author's set
of early page proofs (before the title-page etc. was printed: Preface and
text only). The proofs are corrected throughout in the author's hand
and have additional poems by him; an extra verse on p. 17; additional
poems on pp. 18, 24 and (25)—the last poem was not printed. Yeats'
Preface is corrected in Yeats' hand. With a holograph letter, dated
"11.x.23" to George Redding presenting the proofs: "You may care to
have Yeats' Preface with his corrections on the proofs. I have added
my verses—so, whether the book appears or not, you at any rate will
have my book with more in it than will appear eventually—and that's
what I care about. Ever yours, Oliver St. J. Gogarty." A unique item
of very considerable appeal.   £450

Another association item in that catalogue merits description:

82 AS I WAS GOING DOWN SACKVILLE STREET. A Phantasy
in Fact. *Rich & Cowan*, 1937. A very interesting book by this
extraordinary author, surgeon, senator, playwright, champion athlete
and swimmer. Henry Morris Sinclair brought proceedings for libel
concerning this book, alleging that two passages in it were defamatory
of him; Samuel Beckett gave evidence for the plaintiff. This is an
association copy having belonged to George Redding, a good friend
of Gogarty, with the signature "G.W. Redding" on the rear end-paper.
A reporter for the *Irish Times* stated: "Redding told me that the verses
which caused the famous libel action . . . were written by himself."
Original green cloth marked.   £10

Finally a book which I was reluctant to see go:

80 SELECTED POEMS. With Forewords by A.E. (George Russell)
and Horace Reynolds. *Macmillan, New York*, 1933. Presentation copy
inscribed by the author to George Redding: "To my Staunch friend
George, stout son of the Muses, from his old friend Oliver. Dublin:
August, 1933." Some small MS. corrections by the author and one
comment in his hand; tear in the margin of p. 153 where there is a
small textual alteration. Last verse of poem on p. 166 deleted by the
author and a MS verse substituted. Fine copy in torn d.w.   £45

Oliver St. John Joseph Gogarty was born on 17 August 1878, the son of Dr. Henry Joseph Kelly Gogarty and Margaret (née Oliver). His birth took place at 5 Rutland Square, East (now known as Parnell Square) in Dublin. The family were well-to-do and lived very comfortably in the tall, red-brick Georgian house, with a number of servants. His father also purchased an attractive country house in Glasnevin, called Fairfield, standing in spacious grounds bounded by a stream. Gogarty later wrote about this country retreat:

> Fairfield House was two stories high with a gable in the middle and a hall door in a rounded tower at one end. Another tower half as high led into the garden . . . . Behind the house was the most wonderful garden I ever saw. A huge yew hedge many hundreds of years old separated it from the kitchen garden. Fully grown yew trees sheltered it from the north . . . .

Dr. Henry Gogarty died from appendicitis in 1891, apparently leaving his widow in comfortable financial circumstances. There was a change for Oliver however, because he left his Richmond Street School for Mungret, an Irish provincial school near Limerick run by the Jesuit Fathers, and then Stonyhurst College, an English Catholic School sited in Lancashire's Ribble Valley. He was there for five years but detested the place; fifty years later he still spoke of it as 'the accursed Stonyhurst on the Pendlehurst Range.' He considered it 'a religious jail.' When he left Stonyhurst he had a year before entering university and his mother sent him to Clongowes Wood, a Jesuit school in Kildare; this was the leading Catholic school in Ireland, and Oliver was happy there. He played cricket and football for the school teams and was regarded as being an outstanding athlete; he also played in the Irish Cup for the Bohemians team and won a gold medal. J. J. Horgan, a classmate of his at Clongowes, recalled him as being 'the most popular boy in the school with his soft voice, witty tongue and pallid handsome face.'

After leaving school he went to the Royal University to study medicine, and then entered the medical school at Trinity in the autumn of 1898. To James Joyce, Trinity was 'a dull stone set in the ring of the city's ignorance,' but it had some leading scholars such as Palmer, Tyrrell and J.P. Mahaffy. Oscar Wilde said it was at Trinity that he learned of 'the aesthetic standpoint to life, and how to love Greek things.' Gogarty's first biographer, Ulick O'Connor, painted a picture of him at this time:

He is of average height, five feet nine, but appears taller because of his athletic figure. There is a slight effect of broadness about the face, but this is an illusion, as a sculptor's callipers have shown that it is a long narrow head of the northern type. The eyes are striking, vivid blue, so deep in colour that his daughter actually remembers their being a shade of violet at times. His hair is brown, but sometimes streaked with gold from the bleaching of the sun, and inclined to stand upright when brushed sideways. There is a fine sweep to the forehead, broad without being over-intellectual; his features are regular, but the nose is slightly large, a characteristic of the Irish face . . . .

Ulick O'Connor also commented: 'Gogarty was taken up by the Fellows in a way that no other student had been since Oscar Wilde was at Trinity. Tyrrell, Mahaffy and Macran invited him to dinner at their houses, and to parties which they gave in their rooms at Trinity. They filled his capacious memory with classical poetry, Virgil, Ovid, Catullus, Horace, Pindar, Aeschylus, Homer, Theocritus, Martial, Moschus, Bion. His quick brain enabled him to rival them in apt quotation, a pastime at which they excelled . . . they valued him for his personality, his wit and charm, his gaiety, which bubbled out of him when some humorous thought or fancy entered his mind . . . . Mahaffy's friendship with Gogarty continued after his pupil had gone down from Trinity. In later years he used to come to fish at Gogarty's place in the west of Ireland. Augustus John recalled with a gleam, that Mahaffy was the only one who could keep Gogarty quiet. ' "Silence Gogarty" he would say if he was concentrating on his fishing, and Gogarty's fountain flow of talk would dry up instantly . . . .'

Gogarty's friendship with James Joyce (immortalized by Joyce using him as the character 'Buck Mulligan' in the opening chapter of *Ulysses*) began when they were introduced in the National Library in 1901. Gogarty was amused by the younger man's mocking gravity, and celebrated his wayward-ness in a limerick:

> There is a young fellow named Joyce
> Who possesseth a sweet tenor voice
> He goes to the Kips
> With a psalm on his lips
> And biddeth the harlots rejoice

In 1903 Gogarty took his B.A., gaining the Vice-Chancellor's Prize with a poem titled 'The Death of Shelley'; also (urged on by Joyce) he won the Royal University's Gold Medal for English Verse, which he promptly pawned.

With the idea of entering for the Newdigate Prize, Gogarty spent two terms at Oxford in 1904. While there he made a number of new friends including Christopher Stone, Compton Mackenzie, Samuel Chenevix Trench, and Dermot Frayer who shared his consuming interest in poetry. He tried various plans to inveigle Joyce to Oxford but these were unsuccessful; he also wrote Joyce a number of letters including one about his failure with the Newdigate:

> This Danaan Druid, O Wandering Aengus, obtained but 2nd place in the Newdigate! Further cause for impecuniosity. My Alexandrines I think are not traditional—hence these tears—Damn tradition and the impenetrability of Professors' souls . . . . However, good luck . . . O Aengus of the Birds. Sing sweetly so that the stones may move and build a causeway to Oxford . . . .

It was in July 1904 that Gogarty first mentioned to G.K.A. Bell that he was trying to rent from the War Office the Martello Tower at Sandycove, commanding a view of Dublin Bay. He proposed to live there for a while with Joyce: 'He must have a year in which to finish his novel. I'll send photos when we house the bard securely. The Tower stands on a high rock over the sea.' The deed of covenant for the Tower was executed on Gogarty's birthday in 1904 but Joyce was not in the group—consisting of Gogarty, Trench and James Starkey—which moved into it in August. Joyce stayed there for a short time in September but quarreled with Gogarty and left, writing to Starkey from Cabra on 15 September: 'My trunk will be called for at the Tower tomorrow (Saturday) between 9 and 12. Kindly put into it a pair of black boots, a pair of brown boots, a blue peaked cap, a black cloth cap, a black felt hat, a raincoat and the MS of my verses which are in a roll on the shelf to the right as you enter. Also see that your host has not abstracted the twelfth chapter of my novel from my trunk . . . .'

That Gogarty did not take his medical exams very seriously was shown by a jape in Dublin when he arrived at the Examination Hall in a shutter-drawn cab from which he emerged blindfold to be led into the Hall, a stratagem, he explained, to avoid his seeing a certain red-haired person whom he considered his hoodoo. Perhaps not surprisingly he failed the exam but was allowed to continue his clinical studies. The so-called Richmond Hospital which Gogarty attended in fact comprised three hospitals, with many upsetting sights to be seen. Dr. J.B. Lyons, Gogarty's second biographer, commented: 'Festering wounds, unalignable fractures, and the stink of osteomyelitis were surgical commonplaces while in the medical wards the rapid cachexia of diabetes, the wasting fever of pulmonary tuberculosis, the choking terror of diptheria, the enervation and *café-au-lait* pallor of endocarditis, the progressive languor of pernicious anaemia presented heart-rending sights. Syphilis, the most versatile of diseases, was to be encountered daily in one or other of its three stages, the early genital sore, the widespread rash with "snail-track" mucosal ulcers which developed some weeks later, or the depredations of the tertiary phase in bones, blood-vessels, and brain.' Not surprisingly Gogarty adopted a professional shell of detachment, and in *Ulysses* Joyce makes 'Buck Mulligan' speak airily of death:

> And what is death, he asked, your mother's or yours or my own? You only saw your mother die. I see them pop off every day in the Mater and Richmond and cut up into tripes in the dissecting-room. It's a beastly thing and nothing else. It simply doesn't matter.

Gogarty was mixing in Dublin's literary circles, meeting authors such as George Moore and W.B. Yeats who became a life-long friend. But the salient events of 1906-7 Gogarty compressed into a sentence written to Dermot Freyer: 'As to me I have been in America since I wrote to you; I got qualified, married; and I have an only begotten son in whom I am well pleased.' His marriage, after a swift courtship, was to Martha Duane of Rossdhu, Moyard, Co. Galway. Their first son, Oliver Duane Odysseus Gogarty, was born on 23 July 1907. Gogarty passed his final examinations in June 1907, having much benefited from instruction by Sir Robert Woods, a well-known ear, nose and throat specialist. Woods encouraged him with the remark: 'There will be enough in my back-wash, Gogarty, to keep you going for the rest of your life.'

In the autumn of that year Gogarty and his wife went to Vienna, leaving their son with a nurse at 17 Earlsfort Terrace in Dublin. They rented rooms which had once belonged to Krafft-Ebing. Gogarty liked the atmosphere of Vienna and found it a good place to obtain surgical practice. He returned to Dublin in March 1908 and specialised in ear, nose and throat surgery like his mentor Woods.

On 23 February 1911 Gogarty applied for a post in the Meath Hospital and was duly elected, remaining on the staff there for the rest of his medical career in Dublin. All of his colleagues testified to his brilliance as a surgeon. 'Gogarty was extraordinarily dextrous. He was like lightning with his hands,' Surgeon Lane of the Meath Hospital remembered.

The Gogartys had two more children: another son, Dermot, born in 1908 and a daughter, Brenda, in 1912. Gogarty took a great interest in them and was particularly anxious to nurture any athletic ability, teaching them to swim at an early age.

Fairfield House was sold in 1912 but in 1917 Gogarty acquired another country house named Renvyle, situated on the edge of the Atlantic in Connemara where the climate was moderated by the Gulf Stream. Augustus John, who visited the house on more than one occasion and painted Gogarty's portrait, enthused over the landscape, calling it the most beautiful in the world. The ancient house was built in an H-shape with some walls being more than six feet thick. It looked out on to a beach and was close to two lakes. To it came Yeats, an early visitor, and Lord Tredegar, Lady Leslie, Lady Lavery, Viscountess Castlerosse, Mrs. Valentine Fleming (Ian Fleming's mother), Lord Beaverbrook, Lady Leconfield and many other distinguished guests.

There was much poverty in Ireland at this time and behind the splendours of the Castle and Georgian houses in Dublin there were frightful slums. Gogarty's medical duties often brought him into contact with terrible living conditions and he wrote a play about tenement life, *Blight*, which opened at the Abbey Theatre on 11 December 1917, though his name did not appear on the programme because he used the pseudonym 'Alpha and Omega.' 'Omega' was Joseph O'Connor who had helped Gogarty to revise some of the dialogue. The critic for the *Independent* wrote: '*Blight* is the tragedy of Dublin—the horrible, terrible, creeping crawling spectre that haunts the slumdom of the capital of Ireland. It is not horror for horror's sake. That charge may not be levelled against the authors with any hope that it may be maintained, for if I understand aright the meaning of the painters of this lurid picture it is this: Slumdom is the nest of vice; charity as a palliative is no cure. The charity in fact that endows the hospitals and helps those institutions to extend their premises and cater for increased cases is misdirected charity. Away with the seat of the disease!' The play dealt mainly with the life of a Dublin labourer Stanislaus Tully who was awaiting a court award for injuries incurred while working. When he won the case he was corrupted by the money and became a slum landlord himself.

Gogarty's second play, called *A Serious Thing*, was produced at the Abbey Theatre in August 1919, again using a pseudonym, 'Gideon Ouseley'. Ostensibly dealing with the Roman occupation of the Holy Land in the Augustan Age, it was a satire on British rule in Ireland. Gogarty was an early supporter of Sinn Fein and a staunch friend of Arthur Griffith and Michael Collins; his house in Ely Place was always open to Collins who slept there several times during the Black-and-Tan period. Richard Mulcahy, then chief-of-staff of the IRA, wrote: 'Gogarty's house was a valuable meeting ground for people of different beliefs and creeds. It was particularly valuable for Arthur Griffith who could meet there on terms of social intercourse, Unionists and landed gentry who differed from him in political principle but who had the common good of Ireland at heart.'

As a Senator and supporter of the Irish Free State, Gogarty had a number of enemies among those who were not willing to accept the treaty with the British; after they failed to kill him they burnt Renvyle House to ashes, destroying many of his most precious possessions including paintings by Augustus John and Sir William Orpen. 'Nothing left but a charred oak beam quenched in the well beneath the house. And ten tall square towers, chimneys, stand bare on Europe's extreme verge.'

For a while Gogarty lived in London, with consulting rooms in Grosvenor Street, but returned to Dublin weekly. His wife could not be persuaded to leave Ireland even temporarily. Lady Dunsany commented: 'She has married a charming flibbertigibbet and a sacrifice is required if she is to keep him.' Shane Leslie referred to his sojourn in London: 'His conversation was a nine-day wonder. All the leading hostesses vied to have him at their dinner-parties and "At Homes".'

When Gogarty was being swept along in the River Liffey he had vowed he would present the river with swans if he were saved. He did this on 26 April 1924 and the little ceremony was witnessed by a small but distinguished group which included Yeats, Lennox Robinson and W.T. Cosgrave, President of the Irish Free State.

His writing and various other activities gradually began to divert Gogarty from the medical world. He joined the Irish Aero Club and became Ireland's first medically-qualified pilot. At the Taillteann in 1928 he came third in the archery competition and won the gold medal for poetry with his book *An Offering of Swans*. During the week following the Taillteann Yeats crowned Gogarty with a wreath of bay leaves and said in a speech: 'One book seemed at once pre-eminent, by Dr. Gogarty, who, like Henry James, discovered his genius in contemplating with the eyes of a stranger, and so with clear eyes, what seemed most beautiful in the life of England . . . .' The Cuala Press edition of the book was the first to reach the general public since both *Hyperthuleana* and *The Ship* had been privately issued in very small editions. George Moore wrote: 'I like extremely the poems you sent me. They are the best you have done and they encourage me to believe you have come into your complete talent at last . . . .' John Eglinton wrote in *The Irish Statesman*: 'There is a lightness and transparency about Senator Gogarty's lyrics as if they were carved out of compressed air . . . .' and A.E., reviewing the English edition, commented 'The wit that used to delight his friends is here carved and polished more delicately and given a soul of bravery or light Melancholy.' Two poems from the book were included in *The Oxford Book of English Verse*, edited by Sir Arthur Quiller-Couch.

For a few years Gogarty spent a good deal of his spare time in flying and had a number of minor adventures. On one occasion when landing he killed a sheep; he wrote about this to Lady Londonderry: 'I hit an unsaleable sheep. I said "The Government's policy is right." Then I knew I had concussion of the brain.' The government he referred to was that of Mr. de Valera, one of his political opponents. Gogarty also wrote to Harford Montgomery Hyde in 1934 about taking part in an air display over Ards airport: 'I'm rather limited in my stunts, but if you see a Moth plane, blue IU, coming from the South, along the west border of Strangford Lough at 4000 feet, it will be mine. All I can do is to lose height by half a dozen spins, a loop or two, and a landing (this last, I hope, shall not be exceptional).' Professor Mario Rossi, who visited Gogarty at Renvyle after it had been rebuilt, wrote a book about Ireland, describing his host as 'a Renaissance prince, the great host, the all-round man, surgeon, poet, conversationalist, senator, playwright.' Gogarty wrote a letter to Rossi, saying he was pleased to have this compliment but he was unable to induce his bank manager to consider him in the same princely context.

After the publication of *As I Was Coming Down Sackville Street*, Henry Morris Sinclair commenced proceedings for libel against Gogarty in February 1937. There was a passage on page 71 of the book which referred to an old userer whose habit was to entice small girls into his office for sexual amusement, going on to say that the userer had grandchildren who had inherited this predilection for the immature. 'Sinclair claimed that he could show that his grandfather had been accused of procuring small girls and interfering with them and that, therefore, he was identified by the passage in the book as one of the grandchildren who, it was suggested, indulged in similar practices.' The statement of claim also referred to verses on page 65 which the plaintiff claimed libelled him. In an affidavit Sinclair alleged that Gogarty's book was 'a reservoir of filth and the grosser forms of vulgarity.' The hearing commenced in Dublin's High Court on 22 November 1937. Samuel Beckett was a witness for the plaintiff and his credentials as a writer were challenged by Gogarty's lawyer, J.M. Fitzgerald. Mr. Justice O'Byrne commented on Beckett: 'You saw the witness in the witness-box, and I have no doubt but that you will be able to apprise very accurately the amount of weight which you ought to attach to his testimony. He did not strike me as a very satisfactory witness . . . .' The jury's verdict favoured Sinclair and he was awarded £900 damages. A regrettable aspect of the case was that it was used by some people to accuse Gogarty of anti-Semitism, whereas he had many Jewish friends and dedicated his book *Elbow Room* to Philip Sayers, a Jewish businessman.

An accusation which can be more fairly levelled at Gogarty was that he often spoke impulsively and considered derision to be in order if witty. Someone once said about him to Mrs. Yeats: 'at this minute he's sitting somewhere saying scandalous things.' She replied: 'And don't you know that a man can do that and still be the most loyal friend you ever had.'

When Gogarty sold his fine Dublin house, 15 Ely Place, to the Royal Hibernian Society it was a sign that his medical career was coming to a close. He told his friend Shane Leslie, 'The Senate cost me my practice.' He began to spend more time in Connemara, toiling to the summit of Croagh Patrick and sailing to Caher Island during the time he was writing *I Follow Saint Patrick*.

In 1938 Harford Montgomery Hyde was responsible for bringing a libel to Gogarty's attention. In an unpublished journal he wrote: 'I had wired Gogarty to come over to London as he had been libelled by Patrick Kavanagh in *The Green Fool*—K. said G. kept a mistress at his house in Dublin. K. who called there, mistook the white robed maid for the lady in question, with whom he considered every poet in Ireland was provided. We lunched, on Derby Day, June 1, 1938, with Frank Owen and discussed the case.'

In 1939 Gogarty sued the publishers and printers of *The Green Fool* for defamation of character: the case was heard in London on 21 March and Gogarty was awarded £100 damages and costs. He celebrated his victory the next day by lunching with Sir William Rothenstein who described him to Enid Starkie as 'a joyous, wise libidinous companion, with a Rabelaisian note, which I like.'

An important literary event occurred on 4 May 1939—the publication of James Joyce's book *Finnegans Wake*. Gogarty's review of it appeared in the *Observer* a few days later. His attitude to it was ambivalent but he found much to praise:

> When I think of the indomitable spirit that plodded on, writing *Ulysses* in poverty in Trieste, without a hope of ever seeing it published, I am amazed by the magnitude of this work, every word of which in its 628 pages, twisted, and deranged in order to bring up associated ideas in the mind. The immense erudition employed, and the various languages

ransacked for pun and word-association is almost incredible to anyone unaware of the superhuman knowledge the author had when a mere stripling. In some places the reading sounds like the chatter during the lunch interval in a Berlitz school. Every language living and dead in Europe gabbles on and on . . . .

Later in the year the Cuala Press published Gogarty's *Elbow Room*. The eponymous poem described an attic 'in the vault of Space,' a not very inviting place but one which would at least give him relief from his present environment:

> Oh! what a place to speak your mind
> Without disquieting mankind!
> There's where I find elbow room
> Alone, beyond the crack of doom.

By this time Gogarty's children were grown up and self supporting; his wife was happy running the Renvyle House Hotel. Gogarty felt free to do exactly as he wanted. He volunteered to join the RAF but was rejected because he was too old. In September 1939 he flew to America and began a lecture tour. He was much taken by various aspects of the country, including its vastness:

> The trees, rivers, and mountains of America delight me. Even though the inhabitants have not as yet dominated the landscape (it is the other way round just now), signs are not wanting that the landscape is entering into American literature. The trees of America are more varied than those of the Old World . . . . Of trees in bloom who can speak? Acre after acre of apple orchards in bloom—a sight that can hardly be sustained such is the joy it transmits . . . .

Best of all he liked Manhattan which he described as 'the lordliest Venice of the world':

> Venice with its far-famed Giotto's tower, what is it to the towers of New York? It is beaten even for very grace. This tower town is unequalled in the mind of man . . . . There is the Ritz Tower, Beekman Tower, Waldorf Tower and Tudor and Windsor Towers. Towers and towers and towers to the lofty sky . . . . How well they balance each other, these soaring pavilions of the sky. The loveliest building on earth is the Chrysler building . . . .

For a while Gogarty stayed at the Ritz Tower and then at the Beekman Tower, but after deciding to become an American citizen he rented an apartment at 45 East 61st Street, pleasantly situated between Madison and Park Avenues, and within strolling distance of Central Park. Asked about returning to Ireland, he said 'Why should I? In Dublin I'd spend most of my time sitting in pubs talking to people for nothing. Here I make a comfortable living saying the same thing for money.'

Mad Grandeur, which he published in 1941, was a historical novel, a kind of eighteenth-century tableau. His friends in New York at this time included Professor André Michalopolus, Dr. William Spickers, Mrs. Mary Owings Miller and Harford Montgomery Hyde, then a major in the Intelligence Corps.

Gogarty stayed in New York during the war but made two return trips to Ireland between 1945 and 1948. In 1948 he began an autobiography, *It isn't this time of year at all*, but this was not published until 1954. His collected poems were published in 1952, in a limited edition of 500 copies, with prefaces by Yeats and A.E. Ian Hamilton, in his review in the *Manchester Guardian*, wrote that 'Yeats himself had something to learn from Gogarty whose love of the natural world is a rare frenzy and who seldom succumbs to the English curse "of mixing philosophy up with verse".'

Living in New York was Gogarty's own choice but at times he seems to have been a rather sad, lonely man in his last years. Speaking at the International James Joyce Symposium in Dublin in 1977, Denis Johnston said, 'In his latter days he became—I was going to say a pathetic figure but you couldn't possibly regard Gogarty as pathetic—but he was a figure that was, as it were, losing faith in himself and it's understandable that he began to do that business of repeating himself in one book after another . . . falling to some extent into a rut in a downtown district of New York where one would sometimes meet him and he would join you in a pub on Third Avenue. This was, I think, the saddest period of his life because he was alone . . . .'

In 1956 Gogarty made his last trip to Ireland, still fulminating against De Valera. Apparently it was during this visit that he made up his mind to retire to Ireland at the end of the next year, but that was not to be. On 18 September 1957 he collapsed and was taken by ambulance to the Beth Israel Hospital, a massive building between 1st and 2nd Avenues providing for the teeming Lower East Side. Gogarty had been born with a caul and had had his share of good luck, but this had run out. In the hospital he was talking to a writer friend, Ben Lucien Burman, when he went pale and said, 'I think my trouble is coming on me.' He died during the morning of 22 September 1957.

His body was flown to Shannon airport and then taken by a hearse northwards to Galway and Connemara; overnight the coffin was placed in Letterfrack Church. He was buried at Ballinakill cemetery, on a green hillside, close to Shanbollard Lake. William Cosgrave, first President of the Irish Free State, attended the funeral. A lone swan moved towards the centre of the lake and Monsignor Browne chanted in a low voice:

> *Mein lieber Schwan—ach diese letzte traurige Fahrt*
> (My beloved swan. Now for our last sad journey)

Gogarty's tombstone is engraved with the first verse of his poem, 'Non Dolet':

> Our friends go with us as we go
> Down the long path where Beauty wends,
> Where all we love foregathers, so
> Why should we fear to join our friends?

10. ——— *ROBERT GATHORNE-HARDY* *& The Mill House Press*

It was the urbane P.H. Muir who suggested that I should contact Robert Gathorne-Hardy about the books he produced at the Mill House Press. Percy Muir's conversation was often witty—it was always informative; occasionally he would proffer advice and I listened intently. During a visit to the Elkin Mathews office, then at Takeley, in 1952 I told Percy that I liked the Mill House Press books because they were obviously genuine examples of a private press, idiosyncratic and with amateurish faults. Percy said that I should call in at Stanford Dingley, adding 'you're practically neighbours.' This was an exaggeration, but it was true that our cottage and office were situated a few miles to the east of Reading while the Mill House, Stanford Dingley, stood on the banks of the River Pang perhaps a dozen miles to the west.

Immediately on returning to Hurst I wrote to the owners of the Press asking if I could call in one day, and received a friendly reply. Memories of that far off visit are few but I know that I had a pleasant impression of both Gathorne-Hardy and his life-long friend and partner, Kyrle Leng. On a second visit, a few weeks later, I took my wife and this was treated as more of a social occasion during which we were shown round the garden and grounds down to the Cyclamen wood near the mill-race of the Pang.

We soon found out that the garden was Gathorne-Hardy's pride and joy. The house seemed damp and rather scantily furnished, with a great pile of wood-ash in the fireplace; there were a few relics of Edward Fitzgerald and splendid paintings on the walls. The two bachelors made it obvious that they preferred to be out of doors. Here is an abbreviated description of part of their grounds from Gathorne-Hardy's book *Three Acres and a Mill* (Dent,

1939): 'I went into the water-meadow, which forms one end of our quarter-of-a-mile long, river-margined, narrow little estate. Seven years ago we planted it with trees, and it was beginning to look like a wood. And though our plans for enlivening the river bank were still more than half a dream, here I knew, on the water's edge, were healthy bulbs of the Loddon lily, and, in a treeless area, many invisible daffodils; and close to the house, divided from it by a little bay where the cattle used to drink, dead twigs recalled the burnt-out glories of purple loosestrife and yellow.'

The partners of the press also kept bees, and we were offered mead to drink. Among the press ephemera they gave us was a letter-heading for 'PURE ENGLISH HONEY 2 lbs weight From Kyrle Leng: The Mill House Stanford Dingley Berkshire,' decorated with a delightful old wood engraving. They seemed keener on looking out ephemera to give us than selling us books, and this early impression did not change over the next twenty years; they had many talents but neither of them could be described as a business man.

The Honourable Robert Gathorne-Hardy was born on 31 July 1902; he was the third son of the Earl of Cranbrook and Lady Dorothy Boyle. As a boy he became interested in geology and botany, the latter becoming a lifetime interest. He was educated at Eton and Christ Church, Oxford. At the age of eighteen he met Kyrle Leng and they remained friends until Leng's death in 1958. At first Gathorne-Hardy studied medicine at university but eventually he took a degree in Law. He did not persevere long with a legal career but joined the staff of *The Gramophone* when it was edited by Compton Mackenzie and Christopher Stone. From his early years Robert G.-H. was a book collector with a penchant for the works of Jeremy Taylor whose bibliography he compiled much later. Percy Muir, in his entertaining book of reminiscences *Minding My Own Business* (Chatto & Windus, 1956), described Gathorne-Hardy's first encounter with the then wizard of the antiquarian book world, A.W. Evans, in the London premises of Elkin Mathews Ltd., situated at No. 4a Cork Street, W.1: 'Young Robert Gathorne-Hardy, in 1924, found the shop was on his route home from the office of *The Gramophone* . . . . He dropped in, prepared to find the usual discouraging or disparaging response to his inquiry for the works of such divines as Richard Baxter, Bishop Hall and Jeremy Taylor. Instead he found a knowledgeable enthusiast able and willing to swap quotations, with original editions at hand from which to verify them.'

A.W. Evans asked R.G.-H. to join Elkin Mathews but Robert countered this with the suggestion that his elder brother, the Hon. Edward, should fill the vacancy. Percy Muir's first reaction to Edward G.-H. was not favourable: 'I disliked this very superior, willowy young man, with his long wavy hair, which constantly fell over one eye, the shrug with which he constantly thrust it back, his cordless, rimless monocle, his languid Oxford-accented speech, and his general Bloomsburyism. Especially irritating was the confident manner in which he frequently challenged certain cherished shibboleths of the trade and the irritation was not modified by the off-hand manner in which he established his shocking heresies . . ..' However this antagonism quickly diminished and they became friends. Soon afterwards Robert G.-H. also joined the firm.

It was in 1925 that the Mill House was acquired: 'I was at work on my first job in London, when one day Kyrle came to me, saying that he had heard of a house in a village, on one of the tributaries of the Thames . . . . The house dated from 1870. It was well built, but very ugly. The slate roof, the blue-and-red patterned walls, the festoons of carved wood under the eaves, the formlessness of it—these just made a typical piece of mid-Victorian suburbia, plumped down incongruously in a rural village . . ..' However the friends were won over by the grounds and the convenient situation of the house, and in the following year they issued the first of the Mill House Press publications: *Village Symphony* by R.G.-H., in an edition of 15 copies printed on a toy Adana press. Their project for 1927 was more ambitious, *My own life* by David Hume, and they purchased an old Albion hand-press in order to print it.

A chance encounter in 1928 was to change R.G.-H.'s life: he described it in his book *Recollections of Logan Pearsall Smith* (Constable, 1949): 'My brother Eddie was a partner, senior to me, in the same business. We worked, at separate desks, in a large book-walled room on the first floor . . . . One day I heard a slow shuffling step, as a customer came upstairs into the room. Then, in a quiet, rather shy voice he asked Eddie, "Have you got any first editions of Jeremy Taylor?" . . . I saw a largish man with a stoop which disguised his height; it wasn't so much that he appeared fat, as that his weight seemed too much for his strength. His back and shoulders were curved; his neck apparently crushed down by his head against his shoulders. His spectacles rested on a long and pointed nose (the nose so faithfully exaggerated in Max's caricature); his hat was straight on his head, with grey hair showing behind it; his clothes were nondescript and expensively respectable. It might have been a well-to-do elderly clergyman who chose not to wear his clerical collar . . . .'

From this chance meeting a new career evolved for R. G.-H., that of amanuensis, literary collaborator and part-time companion to Logan Pearsall Smith. It continued for some ten years, more or less coming to an end after a mutual trip they undertook to Iceland in 1938 during which Smith was both physically ill and suffering from a mental breakdown. In *Recollections* . . . Gathorne-Hardy wrote: 'The course of his illness was roughly as follows: for about six days he suffered from a normal and progressively more dangerous attack of pneumonia; then his temperature returned steadily to normal, and for about a fortnight he was violently mad; during the last three or four days in Iceland—and for no longer—he was coming back towards his proper senses. In his account of the matter, taking into consideration the time which actually elapsed, he was, he makes out, ill and delirious for nearly a fortnight, and, while admitting his craziness, he lets it be attributed, as a violent delirium, to his fever. The disease, he says, "heated my blood up to that fantastic temperature in which the tongue is not the least controlled by reason, and I began to pour out on those who approached my bedside a flood of vile and gross vituperation." A little later he writes, "When, on the fall of my temperature, reason was once more seated on her throne, the doctor and I had a good laugh over the mad accusations I had brought against him." The recollection of some actual conversation may very likely have prompted the picture, but at no time, of course, while we were still in Iceland, was he capable of discussing reasonably and dispassionately his recent condition.'

Until Pearsall Smith's nervous breakdown, Gathorne-Hardy had found the job with him congenial. He was working on literary projects very much to his own taste, in pleasant surroundings and with an easy-going boss. He also had plenty of free time to write a novel and a book on his foremost interest, *Wild Flowers in Britain*, which was published, with illustrations by John Nash, by Batsford in 1938. Among the more notable publications of the Mill House Press during that period were *Wailing Wall* by M.R. James (1928); *Miss Mew* by Osbert Sitwell (1929); *Conjugal Fidelity: A Suppressed Dialogue Between Boswell & Johnson* (1929); *On Receiving Trivia From The Author* by Robert Bridges (1930); *How Little Logan Was Brought To Jesus* (1934); *The Poems of Gaius Catullus*: Edited by John Carter, with a rendering into English verse by Robert Gathorne-Hardy (1934: an interesting project which was abandoned after only 2 parts had been printed); *The Ten*

Commandments: Drawings by Gilbert Spencer (1934); and *Death in Iceland* by Logan Pearsall Smith (1938).

Robert Gathorne-Hardy and Kyrle Leng both felt strongly that appeasement of Hitler was wrong and promptly volunteered for the Fire Service when war was declared; subsequently they were enlisted in the First Aid Service. In his spare time R.G.-H. did some occasional work for Pearsall Smith, but no Mill House Press publications were issued during the war.

The first post-war booklet was *Seven Poems, Written in War-Time* by R.G.-H.; this was closely followed by *Four Collects* by Robert Bridges. In subsequent years there were attractive editions of *Occasional Memorandums . . .* by Thomas Gray and *Common Chords* by Siegfried Sassoon.

Once we were in touch with the Press we started to catalogue their publications regularly, and other business came about as from time to time we purchased books and manuscripts from the R.G.-H. library. In our Catalogue 25 we described Pearsall Smith's manuscripts and proofs for his edition of *The Golden Shakespeare*, also his (partly unpublished) MSS for *Milton & His Modern Critics*. Less important items figured in many of our catalogues but a full list would make for tedious reading. Items worth mentioning are the R.G.-H. manuscript of the book *Recollections . . .*, and a family copy of a Thomas Lovell Beddoes rarity, the Maria Edgeworth copy of *The Bride's Tragedy* (Dr. Thomas Beddoes married Maria's sister Anne and their son was the poet).

During the time we knew him R.G.-H. never seemed to be particularly well off: I mention this only because of a truly ironic situation at his death. Occasionally he would be keen to raise money for a trip to Italy, where he had a tiny cottage in Amalfi, and at such times he sold books which he said he was loath to see depart, such as Edward Fitzgerald's heavily annotated copy of Lucretius which we described as a postscript to our Catalogue 46. A kind of enjoyable ritual evolved with him in which we spent the morning looking at books and making offers before adjourning for a pub lunch at the Bull Inn just across the road from the Mill House. During these lunches Gathorne-Hardy told us many amusing stories, most of which had been gleaned during his association with Pearsall Smith; there was a particularly funny and scandalous one about Henry James which he was liable to repeat.

In 1958 R.G.-H. suffered a great blow when his friend Kyrle Leng died. He wrote to Percy Muir about this: 'I'd always lived on the assumption, which I knew to be false, that he was likely to live as long as I would. It was wise, I think, & made for a better life . . . . I'm staying on here—there's nothing else to do. It is difficult, and at times terrifying; but I seem to be managing . . . .'

In November of the following year, during a lunch at the Bull, we asked him to write in our private anthology, 'Likes & Dislikes'. He did this without a moment's hesitation:—

Dislikes

Ezra Pound
Advertisements for detergents on I.T.V.
Custard made from powder
Plastic
Dahlias
The New Statesman

Likes

Draught beer in a village pub
Italy (except Milan)
Cyclamen
People
Dogs
Mozart
Cuttlefish

From 1953 we were regular recipients of the Mill House Press pamphlets which R.G.-H. sent out at Christmas. These included *White Sauce*: now first printed from the original manuscript in the handwriting of Edward Fitzgerald; *Cousin Crowe* by Logan Pearsall Smith; and *Walter Pater* by Michael Field and Logan Pearsall Smith. The last one we received came at Christmas 1969 and was sadly prophetic. It was the translation of some lines, in the Neapolitan dialect, dictated on his deathbed by the Marchese di Caccavone (1798-1873):

NOW THAT THE LAMPS ARE GUTTERING LOW

Now that the lamps are guttering low
Revels and banqueting must pass:
Good health to the friends I leave below!
Boy! Lift the glass!

Robert Gathorne-Hardy died on the 11th February 1973 and was buried in his own grounds, in the little wood near the river Pang. By a stroke of

irony he had inherited a large fortune a few weeks before his death so that
a newspaper report of the event was headlined:

AUTHOR'S £1M

Botanist and author Mr.
Robert Gathorne-Hardy, who
died in February aged 70,
left £1,059,228 it was
announced yesterday.

11. —— *THE YELLOW BOOK Volume 1*

'Beware the Yallerbock, my son!
The aims that rile, the art that racks,
Beware the Aub-Aub bird, and shun
The stumious Beerbomax!'
Mostyn Piggott

The inception of *The Yellow Book*, the publication which was to create such a stir in the 1890s, took place on January 1, 1894, a dreary day it seems, when the metropolis was beset by 'one of the densest and soupiest and yellowest of all London's infernalest yellow fogs.' For it was on that day that the twenty-one year old Aubrey Beardsley lunched with Henry Harland at Harland's flat in the Cromwell Road. Years later Harland described the meeting: 'Aubrey Beardsley and I sat together the whole afternoon before a beautiful glowing open coal fire and I assure you we could scarcely see our hands before our faces with all the candles lighted, for the fog you know . . . . We declared to each other that we thought it quite a pity and a shame that London publishers should feel themselves longer under obligation to refuse any more of our good manuscripts . . . . "Tis monstrous, Aubrey," I said. "Tis a public scandal," said he. And then and there we decided to have a magazine of our own. As the sole editorial staff we would feel free and welcome to publish any and all of ourselves that nobody else could be hired to print . . . the next day we had an appointment with John Lane.' Max Beerbohm was an early witness to the event, adding a postscript to a letter he wrote to his friend Reggie Turner: 'John Lane is going to start a quarterly magazine called *The Yellow Book* with Harland as Editor and Aubrey as Art Editor. It is to make all our fortunes . . . .' Arthur Waugh, in his

103 "

autobiography *One Man's Road*, also claimed to have been in 'at the very birth of *The Yellow Book*,' because he lunched at the National Club in Whitehall Gardens on January 3, when Harland and Lane had come there to tell Edmund Gosse of their plans; Waugh wrote about this meeting in his 'London letter' to *The Critic*.

Henry Harland was described by Richard Le Gallienne as ' . . . one of those Americans in love with Paris who seem more French than the French themselves, a slim, gesticulating, goateed, snub-nosed lovable figure, smoking innumerable cigarettes as he galvanically pranced about the room, excitedly propounding the *dernier mot* on the build of the short story or the art of prose.' Although Harland created a fiction about having been born in St. Petersburg the event had, more prosaically, taken place in Brooklyn on March 1, 1861. He matriculated on September 19, 1877 at the college of the City of New York while his family was living at 249 W. 22nd Street in Manhattan. Then his family moved to 35 Beekman Place, at the foot of East 51st Street facing the East River, and Harland later used Beekman Place as the setting for some of his early fiction. In September 1881 he registered as a Divinity student at Harvard University, but left at the end of his first year; it was at Harvard that he began to make literary contacts, often going to the home of Mrs. A.N. Mosher where he met various authors and also William James, the brother of the man who was to be his literary idol. He then travelled for a year in Europe, and on returning to New York took a job as a clerk in a law firm. At this time he was unable to finish any of his many literary projects, but at the age of twenty-two he married Aline Herminie Merriam (on May 5, 1884) and in the following year he completed his first novel, on a Jewish theme, and published it under the title *As It Was*, adopting the pseudonym 'Sidney Luska'.

In a letter to E.C. Stedman, who had become his mentor and unofficial literary agent, Harland gave some of his reasons for using the pseudonym: '. . . I may as well add that one of my reasons for inclining to a Jewish *nom de plume* is an extremely sound one. I know that if a Jew sees the book lying on a bookseller's shelf, and observes that while professing to treat of *Jewish* matters it has been written by so obvious a Gentile as Harry Harland, he will cry, "Why, what does he know about the Jews?" and drop the presumptuous volume in disgust: whereas if the Author's name has a Jewish flavour, he will on the contrary be disposed in its favour . . . . Another thing, I believe, with a Jewish name on the title page, the sale of the book would be vastly increased . . . .' He ended his letter to Stedman: 'You know I *am* almost a Jew. So the deception would not be so very black.'

Harland's second novel, *Mrs. Peixada*, was dedicated to the Surrogate of New York, by whom he was employed; it was quickly followed by two other novels on Jewish themes, *The Yoke of the Thorah* and *My Uncle Florimond*. According to Arthur Waugh, Harland was later to be ashamed of his early novels, calling them 'mes péchés de jeunesse.'

In 1889 Henry & Aline moved to London, living at first in Alfred Place West, Thurloe Square, and then in a flat at 144 Cromwell Road which soon became one of the centres of the London literary world. Henry Harland proclaimed himself to be a Jamesian and Vincent O'Sullivan called him, 'a sort of lemonade Henry James.'

By the winter of 1892 Harland had found a place in the literary set but was suffering from failing health, diagnosed as tuberculosis, writing to Stedman that his work had been seriously affected by his illness: ' . . . I have written nothing but a handful of short stories . . . . I am coming to lose my faith in the *novel* as a form of fiction, and I think of the short-story more and more as the thing desirable . . . .'

Early in March 1893 the Harlands went to stay in Paris where Henry worked on short stories for the new magazine *Black and White*. Edmund Gosse joined them there the next month and Harland led him on a tour of the Symbolist haunts along the Boulevard Saint-Michel. After Gosse had departed Harland went to call on Henry James and wrote to E.G.: 'I saw James on Tuesday, and he thought the world in general rather a poor affair. He asked affectionately, however, about you, and said how much he had enjoyed his Parisian glimpses of you. Then he gave me a copy of his last volume of tales, forbearing to add, "A poor thing, but me own." Indeed he couldn't have said that truthfully, for the stories are extremely remark-able—amongst the best that he has done . . . .'

In May 1893 Harland wrote to Stedman in some distress about repeated rejections of his stories in America. He said that his work fared better in England and gave other reasons for continuing to live there: ' . . . there are reasons of culture, of sentiment; reasons that refer to Art, to Literature, to Human Nature, which I should have to write a volume to establish . . . .'

The Harlands decided to spend the summer of 1893 in Normandy and rented a house in the village of Varengeville, close to Dieppe. Their guests there included Charles Conder (whom Aline described in a letter to Stedman as 'a real genius if ever there was one, a modern Constable . . .'), D.S. MacColl, the art critic, and Alfred Thornton. MacColl wrote in a letter to his sister, 'Harland . . . believes in the "light touch" . . . . He spends his mornings in an attic in a large Jaeger dressing-gown and writes his stories before washing himself. At other moments he lights little bon-fires on the garden walks and cooks potatoes by himself . . ..' MacColl wrote a poem about the temporary residents at Varengeville, including a verse of his host:

> 'ARLAND, a most reclusive gent,
> On literary toils intent;
> Yet would he o'er the flowing bowl,
> Discourse of Nature and the Soul,
> And things less fit for the reporter,
> For half of him was Latin Quarter.

In his book *Memories of the Nineties*, MacColl stated that he had suggested to the group that what was needed was 'a periodical composed of literature and of art independently.' It is possible that his audience in the little house also included Beardsley. That was the year in which Beardsley's genius was shown in his illustrations for *Salomé*, where he also demonstrated his uneasy friendship with Oscar Wilde by introducing O.W. caricatures into four of the illustrations. He had previously drawn a frontispiece for John Davidson's *Plays* in which he caricatured Wilde, Mabel Beardsley, Henry Harland (as a satyr), Richard Le Gallienne, Adeline Genée and Sir Augustus Harris. It was said that Beardsley was getting even with Harris for his having paid for a performance at the Covent Garden Opera House which Harris had oversold. When Davidson's *Plays* was published, a critic for *The Daily Chronicle* took the artist to task:

An Error of Taste

Mr. Beardsley has contributed a frontispiece a propos of "Scaramouch in Naxos" in which one or two well-known faces of the day are to be recognised—an error of taste which is to be regretted.

On March 1, 1894, *The Daily Chronicle* published the artist's rebuttal of this criticism:

An Error of Taste

Sir,—In your review of Mr. Davidson's plays, I find myself convicted of an error of taste, for having introduced portraits into my frontispiece for the book. I cannot help feeling your reviewer is unduly severe. One of the gentlemen who forms part of my decoration is surely beautiful enough to stand the test even of portraiture, the other owes me half a crown.

I am, yours truly,
Aubrey Beardsley

It was in the same month that the publisher's Announcement of *The Yellow Book* Volume 1 was issued. This was stylish indeed, with a Beardsley drawing showing an attractive, exotically behatted young lady examining some books on a tray in front of a bookseller's shop with the bookseller lounging in a doorway wearing, unaccountably, a Pierrot costume. The Announcement set out the magazine's policy: 'The aim . . . of *The Yellow Book* is to depart as far as may be from the bad old traditions of periodical literature, and to provide an Illustrated Magazine which shall be beautiful as a piece of bookmaking, modern and distinguished in its letter-press and its pictures, and withal popular in the better sense of the word. It is felt that such a Magazine, at present, is conspicuous by its absence . . . .'

The list of proposed contributors was impressive but included a few, such as Jean de France, Lance Falconer, Frank Harris and E. Trelawny Backhouse, who never wrote for the magazine. Backhouse, then a student at Oxford, was to become a noted Chinese scholar, lover of the Dowager Empress of China, and the subject of Hugh Trevor-Roper's brilliant biography *A Hidden Life*. Even though the list proved not to be completely accurate it is indicative of John Lane's taste and ambitions.

Arthur Waugh, in his autobiography, later commented: 'There was no sort of hint that *The Yellow Book* was to be the oriflamme of decadence; indeed, if any such suggestion had been made to its publisher, he would have become inarticulate on the spot. For Lane was dreadfully afraid of offending the proprieties, or indeed of causing any annoyance to any person of importance . . . . So the table of contents for the first number of *The Yellow Book* was an ingenious study in compromise; there was in point of fact no real Yellow Book atmosphere; the sly newcomer intended to be all things to all men . . . .'

Soon after they had called on John Lane the youthful editors had paid a visit to Henry James, on a Sunday afternoon, at his flat in 34 De Vere Gardens. James's two-year venture into playwriting had resulted in his rueful admission of defeat, so the mission to enlist his interest came at a good time. Harland offered the Master the lead place in the inaugural issue. In his private journal James recorded: ' . . . in a periodical about to take birth . . . on the most original lines and with the happiest omens . . . to sound the note of bright defiance . . . .' Years later, in a Preface to the New York edition of his 'Works', H.J. wrote: 'The bravest of the portents of that Sunday afternoon . . . . I have yet to mention; for I recall my embarrassed inability to measure as yet the contributory value of Mr. Aubrey Beardsley, by whom my friend was accompanied and who, as his prime illustrator, his perhaps even quite independent picture-maker, was to be in charge of the "art department". This young man, slender, pale, delicate, unmistakably intelligent, somehow invested the whole proposition with a detached, a slightly ironic and melancholy grace. I had met him before, on a single occasion, and had seen an example of his so curious and so disconcerting talent—my appreciation of which seems to me, however, as I look back, to have stopped quite short.'

Another entry in James's journal shows that his story for the magazine, 'The Death of the Lion,' gave him at least one sleepless night. On January 9, 1894 he noted: 'Last night, as I worried through some wakeful hours, I seemed to myself to catch hold of the tail of an idea that may serve as the subject of the little tale I have engaged to write for H. Harland and his *Yellow Book*. It belongs—the *concetto* that occurred to me and of which this is a very rough note—to the general group of themes of which *The Private Life* is a specimen—though after all it is a thing of less accentuated fantasy. I was turning over the drama, the tragedy, the general situation of disappointed ambition—and more particularly that of the artist, the man of letters: I mean of the ambition, the pride, the passion, the idea of greatness, that has been smothered and defeated by circumstances, by the opposition of life, of fate, of character, of weakness, of folly, of misfortune; and the drama that resides in—that may be bound up with—such a situation . . . .'

Max Beerbohm was privy to some of Beardsley's plans for *The Yellow Book*. In a letter to Reggie Turner, post-marked 16 March, he wrote: ' . . . Aubrey has done a *marvellous* picture for the *Yellow B*: "l'Education sentimentale" he calls it. A fat elderly whore in a dressing-gown and huge hat of many feathers is reading from a book to the sweetest imaginable little young girl, who looks before her, with hands clasped behind her back, roguishly winking. Such a strange curved attitude, and she wears a long pinafore of black silk, quite-tight, with the frills of a petticoat showing at the ankles and shoulders: awfully like Ada Reeve, that clever malapert, is her face—you must see it. It haunts me . . . .'

Katherine Lyon Mix wrote about the practical problems that the editors and publisher faced. 'They worried over the details of producing the best possible volume, and busied themselves in choosing type of printing, cloth for the cover of the desired yellow, and paper suited for the reproduction of the art. The Swan Electric Engraving Company was entrusted with the plates, for its craftsmen understood well the new process which made black and white so successful; the printing went to the Ballantyne Press in Covent Garden, which would use a fine grade of hand-made paper . . . .'

A Cambridge undergraduate appears to have been nettled by *The Yellow Book* Announcement for he published in *Granta* a Prospectus for 'The Yellow Boot,' accompanied by a Beardsleyesque drawing: ' . . . *Yellow* as the complexion of the poet and the gold which inspires him. *Boot*, because Art can dispense with all other clothing, and because our contributors, if they get nothing else, may at least hope to get the Boot . . . . *The Boot* will be coy, it will be saucy, it will be cultured—by Goose it will! . . . a boot with style, a boot with finish; a boot to be soled and *rissoled*; a pointed boot and in no sense a tight laced boot . . . . *The Yellow Boot* will not contain any advertisements other than those of its contributors . . . .'

On the morning of April 15, 1894 a number of shop windows in London turned yellow. J. Lewis May, who as a young man worked in the Elkin Mathews & John Lane shop, remembered it well. 'The lad who spent his days in the back office on a high stool was promoted to service in the front of the shop. Frederick Chapman gave him his first lesson in window dressing and they filled the little bow window full of copies of *The Yellow Book*, "creating such a mighty flow of yellow at the far end of Vigo Street that one might have been forgiven for imagining for a moment that some awful portent had happened, and that the sun had risen in the West."' It was natural that the display in Vigo Street should have taken place, but the dazzling daffodil-coloured cloth was also much on view at Mudies, Bumpus and Quaritch, and Walter T. Spencer had insinuated a few copies among his books with Baxter prints and Dickens in parts. Even the usually high-minded W.H. Smith & Sons stocked the first number, rather to the surprise of John Lane.

On the evening of April 15 an inaugural dinner took place in an upper room of the Hotel d'Italia in Old Compton Street, Soho. 'Henry Harland was everywhere at once, dashing about the room, in his friendly American way introducing those who had not met before, and stirring everyone to gay good humour. More people than expected had come, and the editors were hard put to it to find enough places . . . .' Elizabeth Pennell (whose husband Joseph had contributed an engraving 'Le Puy en Velay') was seated between the editors. 'Her husband had just left for Dalmatia, and in his absence she was distinguished by this mark of Beardsley's appreciation and Harland's friendliness.' There were absences: Henry James was abroad and Edmund Gosse was ill, but had sent 'some delightful verses'; 'George Egerton' was also ill but had asked her husband to represent her. Both Hubert Crackanthorpe and Arthur Symons were in Italy, and Richard Le Gallienne was in Liverpool delivering a lecture on 'The Religion of a Literary Man.'

George Moore was present, seated between Olivia Shakespeare and his new collaborator, 'John Oliver Hobbes.' Poets present included John Davidson, Ernest Dowson, Lionel Johnson 'looking years too young for his critical utterances,' Theo Marzials and W.B. Yeats. Among the artists 'the tawny head of Walter Sickert was plainly visible' while Alfred Thornton sat next to Wilson Steer. Sickert was considered to have made the hit of the evening when he said that he ' . . . looked forward to the time when authors would be put in their proper places by being compelled to write stories and poems round pictures which should be supplied to them ready-made by their taskmasters, the artists.'

The literary contents of the first volume demonstrated Harland's flair and acumen. The fifty-page story by Henry James had pride of place but it was ably supported by short stories by Ella D'Arcy, Harland himself, 'George Egerton' and Hubert Crackanthorpe; there were poems by Richard Le Gallienne, William Watson, Arthur Symons, Edmund Gosse and John Davidson. There was also the first act of a play, 'The Fool's Hour,' written by the brilliant woman author 'John Oliver Hobbes' (Pearl Craigie) and George Moore. And the piece by Max Beerbohm which disconcerted so many critics, 'A Defence of Cosmetics.' Beardsley displayed a similarly catholic taste in the 'Pictures' included, with Sir Frederic Leighton, Joseph Pennell, Walter Sickert, Will Rothenstein, Laurence Housman, Charles W. Furse and R. Anning Bell vying with his own work.

Beardsley's striking cover design of a laughing plump woman wearing a domino, accompanied by a masked satyr, caught the public's attention, and many copies were sold on the first day. Then the press delivered a broadside of criticism. *The Times* condemned it as 'a combination of English rowdiness with French lubricity,' and said 'The cover may be intended to attract by its very repulsiveness and insolence.' *The National Observer* was no kinder and managed to find a recherché word for 'yellow': 'Bizarre, eccentric, uncomfortably heavy to the hand . . . the audacious vulgarity and the laborious inelegance of the cover . . . a misarrangement in orpiment . . . nonsensical and hysterical matter.' *Punch's* attitude was summed up in an epigram: 'Uncleanliness is next to Bodliness.' *The Westminster* dismissed Beerbohm's essay as 'pernicious nonsense' and then turned to one of Beardsley's drawings, commenting, 'We do not know of anything that would meet the case except a short act of Parliament to make this kind of thing illegal.' *Punch* dubbed the art editor 'Weirdsley Daubery', 'Awfully Weirdly' and 'Daubaway Weirdsley', saying that his work had been published by 'The Bogey Head.'

It seems that Beardsley revelled in the attacks and Beerbohm too appears not to have minded. He added a postscript to a letter to R. Turner to this effect: 'The World is rude about me this morning, have you noticed? Like Meredith or Keats or any great striker of new notes, I am rejected at first. But so long as I attract notice I am happy—and so long as I can do beautiful work, and have a little following that calls me "Master".'

Harland was annoyed by a review in The Speaker which imagined the editor saying to 'the band of Bodley Head disciples': 'Be mystic, be weird, be precious, be advanced, be without value,' The reviewer also cited contributions by Crackanthorpe, 'George Egerton' and Harland when commenting: 'The three of them seem, if the metaphor may be permitted, like men who should carve at a feather-pillow with knives to make of it a statue.' Harland wrote about this to Lane: 'We are frightfully abused in The Speaker. I am half inclined to think the article libellous—in which case we could make them apologise or pay damages.' Lane's reply is not known but no action was taken. From the same letter it appears that Harland had taken some of the art criticisms to heart since he added, 'Aubrey must modify himself in Vol. II.' Beardsley wrote to Henry James: 'Have you heard the storm that raged over No. 1? Most of the thunderbolts fell on my head. However, I enjoyed the excitement immensely.'

Though Henry James continued to be associated with the publication, contributing a story 'The Coxon Fund' to the second volume, it is clear that he had some reservations. In a letter from Rome on May 28 he wrote to his brother William: 'I haven't sent you The Yellow Book on purpose: and I have been weeks and weeks receiving a copy of it myself. I say on purpose because although my little tale which ushers it in ("The Death of the Lion") appears to have had, for a thing of mine, an unusual success, I hate too much the horrid aspect and company of the whole publication. And yet I am again to be intimately, conspicuously associated with the 2nd number. It is for gold and to oblige the worshipful Harland (the editor).'

Some other authors agreed with James. 'John Oliver Hobbes' wrote to George Moore: 'Harland wants me to write a poem, story, an article, anything, for the next number. I fear I cannot oblige him. The Speaker on The Yellow Book is only too just. I have never seen such a vulgar production . . . .' And Katherine Bradley and Edith Cooper (joint-authors under the name 'Michael Field') reported that when they saw the display in the windows of the Bodley Head they were 'almost blinded by the glare of hell.'

But if its style and notoriety repulsed some people The Yellow Book attracted many more, including a number of would-be contributors. Of course some of the unsolicited manuscripts were useless, but Harland wrote to Lane: 'By post, from an entirely unknown person, a Miss Charlotte Mew, I have received one of the most remarkable MSS. I have ever read. A story, most subtle and imaginative, and done in a wonderful original style. A new *Y.B.* discovery—fully as remarkable as Ella D'Arcy, though in a totally different way.' This story, titled 'Passed', appeared in the second volume.

In May 1894 the Harlands left England for Paris, saying that they needed to escape for a while from the unpleasantness of the attacks on *The Yellow Book*. Mrs. Harland, using the editorial 'we', wrote to E.C. Stedman about this: 'As we have succeeded in spite of their unfriendliness we bear them only the slight grudge and small amount of contempt one cannot help feeling for meanness unspeakable, and we hope with Heaven's help to succeed so much better in our second number, even than in our first, that they will be the laughing stock of the public and *The Yellow Book*. It is impossible to tell you of the bitterness, hatred and malice rife in the London art world—how each big fish lives by devouring the little fishes as fast as they become half big enough to hold their own. It is all so heart-sickening that we are glad to get away from London and out of it for a fortnight, when we shall be obliged to go back again and face the world and the devil a second time . . . .'

Throughout its four year run *The Yellow Book* continued to attract virulent criticism in the popular press, and a newspaper's mistake was to lead to Beardsley's dismissal. On 5 April 1895 Oscar Wilde was arrested at the Cadogan Hotel and taken in a four-wheeler to Bow Street police station. According to one reporter Wilde 'grasped his suede gloves in one hand and seized his stick with the other. Then he picked up from the table a copy of *The Yellow Book* which he placed in security under his left arm.' Actually the book in a yellow binding was a French novel, *Aphrodite* by Pierre Louys, but *The Yellow Book* was better to splash in the paper's largest print. John Lane was on his way to America at the time and when he landed he was handed a newspaper with the headline: 'ARREST OF OSCAR WILDE, YELLOW BOOK UNDER HIS ARM.' At the same time hostile crowds threw stones at the Vigo Street window under the sign of the Bodley Head. Lane sent a cable to his assistant Frederick Chapman, telling him to withdraw all of Wilde's books. And, goaded by Mrs. Humphrey Ward, several authors expressed indignation and asked for Beardsley to be dismissed. The egregious poet Watson summed up their attitude in a telegram: 'WITHDRAW ALL BEARDSLEY'S DESIGNS OR I WITHDRAW ALL MY BOOKS.' The fifth volume of *The Yellow Book* was then at the printers, but Frederick

Chapman recalled it and expunged all signs of Beardsley. Two weeks late, on 30 April 1895, the heavily censored edition appeared. E.F. Benson summed up the situation neatly in a phrase, 'It turned grey overnight.'

Lacking Beardsley's genius *The Yellow Book* was a comparatively dull production visually, yet it survived until 1897. When Volume XII appeared in January that year *The Times* critic commented, 'The principle upon which the *Yellow Book* is edited would seem to be that at intervals of every three months a section of the reading public is seized with a craving for fresh work by Mr. Henry Harland, Miss Ella D'Arcy, and others of the little school of writers whom the Bodley Head has brought into notice. The contributions, therefore, tend to run largely in the same groove, but still, as this is the twelfth issue, one must admit, mindful of the fate of the *Savoy*, that the principle serves its purpose well enough.'

The last volume (XIII) had some twenty-five literary items and eighteen illustrations crammed into its 317 pages, between covers with a design by Mabel Syrett ('Fighting Cocks'). It was late and did not reach the bookstalls until May: this, inevitably, drew a gibe from *The Times*: 'The Yellow Book* though it has outlived its youthful "wildness", keeps up a reputation for eccentricity by producing its April number . . . in May.'

Though some aspects of *The Yellow Book* may have been eccentric it managed to find a fairly wide public for some excellent material, and its fame lives on. Nearly a century later the thirteen volumes are much sought after and the title still echoes in the public's mind, summing up a period.

12. —————————— *JOHN OLIVER HOBBES*

An oblong volume, the size of a cheque book, bound in shiny yellow wrappers, appeared in London booksellers' windows in 1891. It was issued in the Pseudonym Library series, published by Fisher Unwin, with the title *Some Emotions and a Moral*. The book's unusual appearance was matched by its offbeat text which opened with a flash of fin-de-siècle cynicism: 'Ideals, my dear Golightly, are the root of every evil. When a man forgets his ideals he may hope for happiness, but not till then.' The pseudonym 'John Oliver Hobbes' masked the fact that the book was actually written by a young married woman, Mrs. Pearl Craigie. The book had been accepted by Unwin at the suggestion of his reader Edward Garnett, who was not however uncritical of the author's flippancy and cynicism. Pearl Craigie explained her choice of pseudonym, saying, 'I chose the name John because it is my father's and my son's; Oliver because of the warring Cromwell; and Hobbes because it is homely.' She also said that she was an admirer of the philosopher Hobbes and that his rationalism saved her from 'Maudlin sentiments'. Later on she told an American reporter that 'Hobbes was the ugliest name I could think of,' and, when giving a talk at a New York Club, she stated: 'My jealousy of that creature is not to be expressed. However much I enjoy this party I know perfectly well it is not for me but for Hobbes. But for him I should never have been here. I will not say I dislike Hobbes—but even a woman is human.'

Pearl Craigie had already used a pseudonym 'Diogenes Pessimus' when contributing sketches to the weekly paper *Life* under the title 'The Note-books of a Diner-Out.' Soon after publishing her first book she became a Roman Catholic and added two other baptismal names, Mary Teresa, to her own. 'She read herself into the Church,' one of her priest friends, Father

Gavin, S.J., stated. 'Her conversion . . . could not be ascribed to sermons, still less to the attraction and beauty of the Church's liturgy and public services. She became a Catholic by study and conviction, and in obedience to her conscience.'

She took time in producing a fine manuscript, written in violet ink on thick cream-laid paper, of her second novel, *A Sinner's Comedy* (1892). In a letter to her publisher she explained her attitude to writing: 'Of course people read a novel carelessly—for amusement when they are tired of their own environment and seek a change. But the novelist is nonetheless bound to write his unconsidered trifles with the same pains and thought he would bestow on a Philosophical Treatise, with this reservation, that his pains and thought must not be too apparent.'

Edward Garnett, as Unwin's reader, again recommended publication but added: 'The old faults re-appear in perhaps more marked a degree . . . . She sacrifices again and again reality for wit and flippancy . . . . The fact is, as we said, in criticizing *Some Emotions* for T.F.U., Mrs. Craigie is a clever woman with decided limitations. She knows a good deal of life on one side but little on the other and she is too bent on being cynical to write anything great in any way.'

As in the first novel, the characters in *A Sinner's Comedy* are victims of unsatisfactory marriages. Pearl again showed a mordant wit, much like that of Evelyn Waugh in *A Handful of Dust*. Here is her description of the deathbed scene of Lord Middlehurst:

> He did not speak again till just before he died, when he kissed his wife's hand with singular tenderness and called her "Elizabeth". She had been christened Augusta Frederica; but then, as the doctors explained, dying men often make these mistakes.

What had made Pearl Craigie 'bent on being cynical?' She was born in Chelsea, Mass., a village near Boston, on November 3, 1867. She was the daughter of John Morgan Richards, an ambitious and highly successful business man, and Laura (née Arnold), the granddaughter of a famous Presbyterian preacher. Both parents were said to be intelligent, energetic and responsive. Pearl took after them and was very precocious. John Richards had several business interests including the export of American cigarettes and the manufacture of patent medicines, among them Carter's Little Liver Pills. Business reasons made him decide to live in England, and the family settled in London at that time and Pearl's childhood friends were all English. She had an English governess and an additional English tutor, as it were, in Dr.

Joseph Parker, minister of the City Temple, who was a close family friend. At a very early age Pearl wrote little stories and essays for Parker's approval. Much later he was to write of her as a child: 'She could turn you into an epigram in the act of asking you to have another lump of sugar in your tea, and in your answer she could see your character and forecast your doom. She could fit you into six words and do it so neatly you could not get out again.'

The Richards liked living in England and they prospered there. Their establishments became more luxurious and they had three sons and another daughter. Pearl was sent to a boarding school in Berkshire and then to day schools in London before travelling to Paris to be 'finished'. Her father idolized Pearl and was anxious to further her literary career, for he was a keen reader himself and became proprietor of the magazine *Academy*. Pearl emerged from her finishing school a highly accomplished young woman and multi-talented. She was considered to be a brilliant pianist. In May 1886 she was presented at Court.

The following year, aged only nineteen, she married Reginald Walpole Craigie, a young banker related to the Earls of Orford and Cadogan. At first the young married couple took a flat in Marble Arch Mansions and were much to be seen in London social circles. It was the kind of match that fascinated Henry James, and there is a passage in his novel *The Wings of The Dove* (1902) which may have been written with her in mind since he knew the family: 'The tall rich heavy house at Lancaster Gate, on the other side of the Park and the long South Kensington stretches, had figured to her, through childhood, through girlhood, as the remotest limit of her vague young world.'

The Craigie marriage was a disaster. Reginald Craigie was a vain womaniser with a taste for drink and gambling. He liked to admire his own nude body in a bedroom mirror. Pearl was ill on her honeymoon and rarely happy afterwards. Years later she wrote: 'It was like living with a boa constrictor. To hate anyone as I hated him was in itself a torment.'

Partly as a kind of escape from the marriage Pearl turned to writing, contributing to the *Fun* almanack and several magazines. She also studied classics at the University College, London, under Professors W.P. Ker and Alfred Goodwin. She developed a close friendship with Goodwin and it was he, nearly twenty years her senior, who comforted her in her black, almost suicidal, moods. She often left the marital home and lived with her parents at their house in London or at Old Park on the Isle of Wight. It was on the

Isle of Wight that her only child, a son christened John Churchill Craigie, was born on August 15, 1890.

The birth of the child did not improve the marriage: quarrels continued and Craigie once accused his wife of having had the child by Professor Goodwin. In May 1891 Pearl finally left her husband and went to live with her parents. What *was* true of her relationship with Goodwin was that it had been important in training her in research and intellectual discipline. She said, 'Goodwin gave me the benefits of the *Oxford* method.'

Her third book, dedicated to Goodwin, was again published in the popular Pseudonym Library and titled *A Study in Temptations* (1893). This does seem overly artificial and cynical; even the rustics are cynical, a farmer giving his verdict on book-learning and similar fancy ideas: 'The difference . . . so far as I can tell between a man wi' notions and a man without 'em is this—*the man without 'em pays the bill.*'

Pearl Craigie was now permanently established in her parents' home at 56 Lancaster Gate, W.2. which is located just behind the Bayswater Road. She had been married in the old church there which looks out over Kensington Gardens. John Richards entertained a lot, both at Old Park on the Isle of Wight and at the handsome house in Lancaster Gate. His patent medicine business, with such products as Bromo Seltzer, Mrs. Allen's Hair Restorer, Carter's Little Liver Pills and a line of Colgate items, was thriving (Henry James is reputed to have greeted him once with an unfortunate slip of the tongue, 'How are you, Mr. Carter?'). The fashionably furnished salon with its William Morris flowered wallpaper also displayed framed religious mottos and a placard inquiring 'What Would Jesus Say?' When Pearl noticed guests staring at it she would shruggingly say, 'Oh, that's mother's.' Her mother must have been an embarrassment, considering herself to be an emissary from God and sometimes speaking, to the amazement of visitors, to her unseen friends among the prophets of the Bible. A few years later Laura Richards despatched a peremptory telegram to His Eminence on the Throne of St. Peter: 'POPE, VATICAN, ROME. STOP WAR. RICHARDS.' She sent a similar 'STOP WAR' telegram to the King of Spain.

Despite her mother's growing eccentricities Pearl appears to have been content living at Lancaster Gate: she did much of her writing in a bedroom-study on the third floor, where she would dictate letters to her secretary, Zoe Procter. There she wrote a preface to the second edition of *A Study in Temptations* in which she confided that ' . . . it was composed under the strain of bad health, and all of it in circumstances of peculiar anxiety. If the author had written as he felt or thought, the result would have been far from amusing.'

Her next novel, *A Bundle of Life* (1893) was dedicated to Walter Spindler, the artist who supplied the frontispiece portrait to Lord Alfred Douglas's *Poems*. It is said that Spindler was in love with her. There is a self-portrait of Pearl in the character of Lady Mallinger, a young widow who had been married unhappily at eighteen. Lady Mallinger says: 'The world liked my husband; he ate too much, drank too much and made too merry with other people's lives. No one knows what I suffered.' Lady Mallinger is a woman of quicksilver moods: at luncheon she is 'all vivacity, epigram and paradox'; by teatime she is depressed. She complains of being much misunderstood: 'When I am serious, they say I am in low spirits. When I am sincere they praise my hypocrisy.' She likes men but they fall in love with her too easily with ensuing complications. This certainly appears to have been true of Pearl. She had large liquid eyes, a vivacious manner, a slender elegant figure and was always exquisitely dressed. She attracted politicians as well as authors and artists, and could often be seen at society gatherings on the arm of Arthur Balfour, or George Curzon who was to figure a good deal in her life. Edward Garnett reported to Fisher Unwin that he had found *A Bundle of Life* ' . . . better than we thought possible' because it had 'less improbability, less of that smart and utterly wearisome cheap cynicism, less of artificial *narrative* than in her other books.' Garnett concluded that this book was 'more artistic in that it *leaves out* things the other books *put in*.'

Pearl had achieved a kind of notoriety in London's literary world and she was the subject of a little verse in circulation there:

> John Oliver Hobbes, with your spasms and throbs,
> How does your novel grow?
> With cynical sneers at young Love and his tears,
> And epigrams all in a row.

It was about this time that her affair with George Moore began. Years later, in 1922, Moore told Barrett Clark that he had sought her out after Arthur Symons had told him that 'Hobbes' was a woman: 'That—that was a different matter. I saw her some days afterward at the theatre and thought she was amazingly beautiful. Well, one thing led to another, and I fell in love with her.' The relationship with Moore led to literary collaboration with him, making a one-act adaptation from the French of *Journeys End in Lovers Meeting*, which was put on as a curtain-raiser at Daly's and then at the Lyceum Theatre. They also wrote the first act of a play, *The Fool's*

Hour, which appeared in the first volume of *The Yellow Book*. George Moore gave a fictional account of the affair with Pearl in the story 'Lui et Elles' which appeared in 1921, describing a female writer who used the pseudonym 'Mark Anglewood' with whom he worked in the mansion of her wealthy but 'commonplace' parents. The woman 'Agate' (Pearl) in this story welcomed his attentions but never really accepted him as a lover: 'By some word or letter, sometimes even by acts she would dissipate suspicions, I might also say the belief, that my courtship would bring me to her bed. To be quite truthful, she hinted at the beginning that sex relations did not appeal to her, but such hints are so common among women that one attaches no real significance to the confession, or interprets it in the opposite sense, that sex relations are the one thing of interest to them . . . .' (What a chump George Moore was when it came to women!)

In 1894 Pearl wrote to him: 'I seem the feeblest creature in the world: twenty-six years of life have left me with nothing but a desire for rest and a long sleep. Today I paid three long calls and had to talk to ten people on sixty subjects. People teach me nothing . . .. Tired, tired, tired, TIRED!!'

Vincent O'Sullivan, an American writer who lived in London in the 1890s, wrote a highly perceptive study of Pearl Craigie. In another interesting essay, on George Moore, he commented: ' . . . in writing of Moore it is impossible to escape from speaking of Mrs. Craigie. She was Moore's *femme du monde*. Indeed, from the way he lost his head and his foothold in this affair, threw discretion overboard, went up and down London conveying to the most undesirable subjects that his relations with Mrs. Craigie were of the most intimate character, I came to the conclusion that she was the first and perhaps the only *femme du monde* he had ever bagged. There was a time when he would talk of nothing else—sometimes, it is true in terms more or less covered, but too often openly, so that no one at all familiar with the fashionable people of London could fail to gather what he meant. For this he was abundantly laughed at by some, and abundantly censured by others who set up to be disinterested friends of the American woman, and were perhaps simply jealous. But it was Moore's uncontrollable babbling and nothing else which brought about the separation. . . .'

1895 was a year of intense strain for Pearl Craigie as she sued for divorce, and the case of *Craigie v Craigie* opened on July 3. Pearl, backed by her father, employed four lawyers including two Q.C.s. Mr. Murphy, Q.C., opened the case, well aware that he not only had to prove the husband's misconduct but disprove countercharges of condonation and unreasonable delay in petitioning for dissolution of the marriage, stating that the reason it had not come to trial earlier was the wife's reluctance to air sordid details. He said the case was a painful one and that in the first year of marriage Reginald Craigie had 'abused and treated her badly. He had also threatened her with a pistol . . . . In 1890 the respondent had struck the petitioner, and in March 1891 he told his wife he had become acquainted with another woman.' Reginald Craigie entered as evidence some documents including one addressed to his wife in which he claimed that she had given him permission to commit adultery.

Pearl was cross-examined for nearly five hours and fainted in the witness box. The trial was adjourned until the next day when Mr. Edward Carson, Q.C., asked to speak for the respondent. Carson was an extremely shrewd, pragmatic lawyer who only two months earlier had successfully defended the Marquess of Queensberry against Oscar Wilde's libel suit. Carson told the court that he had informed his client there was no way the charge of condonation could be corroborated. On his advice Reginald Craigie had decided to withdraw from the action.

After Pearl had been vindicated and released from her hateful marriage she wrote to Ellen Terry: ' . . . The strain has been very great. I can hardly realise the verdict at present. I feel that the trial is still going on—that it is going on for ever and ever! The sensation is hideous. But I have got my child.' However, when the boy was entered for Eton in 1899 Pearl had to write to A.C. Benson, his house-master: 'With regard to the boy's religious instruction: he may not be brought up as a Roman Catholic. I have the sole guardianship and custody of the child, but the English law is very decisive on *that* point.'

Pearl's relationship with her mother had deteriorated as Laura Richards had become a wildly eccentric woman, obsessed with religion and determined to dominate the household at 56 Lancaster Gate. Every morning Laura, dressed in a robe-like garment, would sing the Lord's Prayer and several hymns, accompanying herself on the harmonium. On the Isle of Wight 'Mama' would go round the garden, sniffing noisily. 'I smell God on every tree,' she would announce in ringing tones. Pearl's sister was driven to the brink of suicide. To the Rev. William Brown Pearl wrote: 'The wonder is not that Dorothy took laudanum but that both of us did not get rid of ourselves long since. That unhappy woman is our curse. It is appalling but true.' It was vital to get away from Lancaster Gate for a while so Pearl made a trip to America, seeing productions of her plays in Philadelphia, Washington, New York and Boston.

Another novel, *The Gods, Some Mortals and Lord Wickenham* appeared in the year of her divorce, first being printed in *The Pall Mall Budget*; once more it was a tale of an unhappy marriage with the hero Dr. Simon Warre trapped into wedlock with a shrewish singer, Anne. This book has been considered to be her best by some critics. Scenes at the dining table may well mirror some of Laura Richards' tantrums at Lancaster Gate: 'Every day she indulged in some wild burst of temper: she was too passionate to be a mere shrew—her wrath was like a stage storm—violent and abrupt, heralded by moonlight and immediately followed by the noonday sun. The servants dreaded her step; Warre suffocated in her presence; the house was a hell.' Simon Warre, like Pearl, found a refuge in the Jesuit Church: 'When it was dark, he would sometimes steal into the Catholic Church in Farm Street, and rest there, undisturbed . . .. He felt that he was in some ways expected, that his place was set ready, that there were loving friends on every side who had been waiting, watching, longing for his approach . . . .' Warre longs for death but will not commit suicide; he takes a post in a colonial hospital and dies there. His friend Lord Wickenham says, 'I envy him, although his body is one with the sands of the sea, and his grief was more then he could tell, and his life, in men's judgment, a failure.'

This was a period when Pearl appears to have been much impressed and influenced by Thomas Hardy's books. She considered *Jude the Obscure* a masterpiece and wrote to him: 'Its greatness goes beyond literature and challenges comparison with works of amazing genius.' To their mutual friend, Florence Henniker, she wrote: 'Its construction is superb; its literary art, classic.' In 1896 Pearl published a novel *The Herb-Moon* with a heroine who was married, like herself, at nineteen. This was more melodramatic and harder to believe than *The Gods* . . . with a husband who goes mad through sunstroke. Hardy's influence has been detected in this book and in a short story 'The Worm that God Prepared,' written in the same year.

This was a time when she was also working on an idea for a play, encouraged by Henry Irving. After completing it in draft form she changed her mind and turned it into an ambitious novel with a Disraeli-like hero, one which she hoped would be her masterpiece. In order to devote herself to the book she cut down on her social life though her parents complained that in doing so she was losing her chances of marrying again. Her father followed his strictures on this subject by stopping her allowance. This led to her taking a flat in Albany and renting a house on the Isle of Wight. She often felt ill and spent days in bed. To the Rev. William Brown, with whom she had a lengthy correspondence, she wrote: 'Art must indeed be a disease . . . . My own sufferings baffle description.'

Vincent O'Sullivan, in his highly perceptive essay on Pearl Craigie, diagnosed a death wish in her: ' . . . Her own explanation of her sickness of life was that she knew too much about human nature. She reiterates this, but is not convincing. The two best letters other than her own in the volume of her life are those of the Duchess of Sutherland and of Owen Seaman, because they both perceived under the surface of her books almost complete abstraction from life as it really is . . . . So far as can be gathered from her letters, her longing for death was a pagan longing, or if you wish, an Old Testament longing, unilluminated by the soft consolations of Christianity. It was a longing for the last protection of our mother earth, to be celled in the grave out of sight of men and women . . . . Many of the saints, from St. Paul onwards, have longed with an immense and sincere longing to finish their pilgrimage, to be dissolved and to be with Christ; but they longed as travellers in a foreign land sometimes yearn for their own country. With her, it was just death as a terminus. She longed for life to cease as one longs for the quieting of a pugging nerve . . . .'

Pearl's novel with a hero (Robert Orange) like Disraeli, *The School for Saints*, was published in 1897. Like Pearl, Orange also had a fondness for the Catholic Church in Farm Street. ' . . . As the two young men crossed the threshold of the Church, the sight which opened before them was like a dream imprisoned in a rock. The dark stone cavernous building, where shadowy forms were kneeling in prayer and praise, seemed a hollow not made with hands, and the light on the high altar shone through the mist of incense as something supernatural yet living and sacred . . . .' The book was a great success both with the public and the critics. The reviewer for the *Athenaeum* found it 'fascinating' and 'fantastic'; he noted that Robert Orange and his friends 'discuss religion with some fervour but they never become tiresome about it, or give the impression that they are preaching at the reader.' In 1897 Pearl was deep in religious studies; she wrote to Lewis Hind: 'I am going "hammer and tongs" at theology. One of the Jesuit fathers is going to instruct me. Which I call a great piece of good fortune. I have always wanted this. Their system of teaching is the finest in the world.'

In 1898 Pearl had a triumph in the theatrical world with her four-act comedy *The Ambassador* which was produced in the summer at the St. James's Theatre. This had a fine cast with George Alexander, the celebrated actor-manager, in the star part, supported by Henry Irving, Fred Terry and Violet Vanbrugh. When summoned by the audience with their calls of

'Author! Author!' and Pearl appeared, resplendent in white satin, there was another call, 'Where's John?' Then the audience realised that she was indeed 'John' and the shouts changed to 'Pretty John'.

The next play, *The Wisdom of the Wise*, produced in November 1900, was less successful. Max Beerbohm, then critic for the *Saturday Review*, expressed general disappointment: 'Why, then is her comedy so dull? The dialogue is as delightful as ever, showering off its innumerable little bright sparks of wittiness and prettiness. But the characters who speak it! They do not exist. They are the vaguest puppets, there to work out the basic idea, precisely through jigging of their joints; they are not human characters to illustrate the idea in a human manner . . ..'

A sequel to *The School for Saints*, published under the title *Robert Orange*, was again welcomed both by reviewers and the general reading public. The *Punch* satirist Owen Seaman, who years later was to publish a parody called 'Robert Porridge', wrote her an appreciative letter: '. . . I think if I did not know you I should be a little afraid of meeting you. There is only George Meredith besides you, that could have written it . . ..' The book began with a display of her theatrical comedy talent with a character named Lady Sara-Louise-Tatiana-Valerie de Treverell making cynical comments like 'You might as well flirt with the Ten Commandments as fall in love with your wife,' but then it developed into a serious politico-religious novel. Here is Pearl's description of the heroine's feelings when the news reaches her that her husband is alive:

> Every feature quivered under the invisible cutting hand of cruel experience. In those sharp moments of introspection she had gained such a knowledge of suffering that fire seemed to have consumed her vision of life, reducing it to a frightful desert of eternal woe and unavailing sacrifice. Partially stunned and partially blinded by misery she felt the awful helplessness and pain of what is sometimes called the second birth when the first true realization comes that the soul is a stranger, a rebel, strong as eternity, weak as the flesh, free as the illimitable air.

In 1902 Pearl sailed, as a guest of Lord and Lady Curzon, to the Delhi Durbar at which Curzon, as Viceroy of India, formally announced the accession of Edward VII. Pearl was accompanied by her friend Owen Seaman; she wrote articles about the Durbar for the *Graphic* in London and *Collier's* in New York.

Henry James's motives in giving Pearl a copy of his wonderful novel *The Wings of the Dove* are indeed Jamesian; perhaps he thought it was the honourable thing to do. Pearl saw herself in the heroine Milly Theale—a beautiful American heiress, apparently consumptive, in London—though the fictional portrait has been generally accepted as James's elegy for his dead cousin Minny Temple (Leon Edel says: 'In the Venetian chapter James relived old memories, not only the long-ago death of Minny Temple, but the wasting illness of his sister, and the violent death—in Venice—of Miss Woolson'). Pearl may have thought she discerned something of herself in Milly; she was quite certain she saw Owen Seaman in the scheming Merton Densher. To the Rev. William Brown she wrote that she had confronted James with her suspicions: 'Henry James has sent me *The Wings of the Dove*. Clearly, the man is meant to be Seaman. It is hard upon him. With James I took the bull by the horns. I said, in acknowledging the book, "I know Densher. But he is far more child-like than you have made him . . . ." The book was a bit too close to the facts. We are given Venice: hints are given of my style of dressing: he makes me out to be suffering from a mysterious incurable malady (a popular delusion) and makes much of the fact that I *look* well. I have no air of the invalid.'

A point that Pearl did not make with James was that 'The tall rich heavy house at Lancaster Gate' was much like her own, and Kate Croy's aunt, called Maud Lowder, was very much like Mrs. Laura Richards. James wrote that Mrs. Lowder would have been: ' . . . an extraordinary figure in a cage or anywhere, majestic, magnificent, high-coloured, all brilliant gloss, perpetual satin, twinkling bugles and flashing gems, with a lustre of agate eyes, a sheen of raven hair, a polish of a complexion that was like that of well-kept china and that—as if the skin were too tight—told especially at curves and corners . . . .' The impecunious newspaperman Merton Densher was over-awed by the 'vast drawing-room' of the Lancaster Gate mansion but he consoled himself in thinking his hostess was 'colossally vulgar': 'He had never dreamed of so much gilt and glass, so much satin and plush, so much rosewood and marble and malachite . . . .'

From 1902 onwards illness and fainting fits were an ever growing feature of Pearl's life. Perhaps the hyper-sensitive Henry James had divined what was to come. Nevertheless, illness did not curtail her social and literary activities. Her closest friend was perhaps the best-known American woman in London, Lady Randolph Churchill, who in New York had been Jennie Jerome. Together they planned a literary periodical which John Lane saw as a successor to *The Yellow Book*; it was called the *Anglo-Saxon Review*. Lady

Churchill was doubtful whether she could make a go of the project and Pearl wrote a letter reassuring her: 'Dearest Jennie, What do you mean by calling yourself uncultured, unliterary & old? You must be "going crazy"—to use our country's cheerful idiom. You are perfectly charming & your judgment in artistic matters is distinguished. These things you know in your heart, already, so I cannot be accused of flattering you . . . .' The first number had some distinguished contributors: Henry James, at the Palazzo Barbaro in Venice, produced a short story 'The Great Condition'; Leon Edel says of this tale: 'A variant on his old stories about women with a "past"; it was based on an idea furnished by one of his conversations with Meredith.' A short 'John Oliver Hobbes' play, 'Osbern and Ursyne,' was also included, along with a poem by Swinburne, an article by the Prime Minister Lord Rosebery, and an article on wireless telegraphy by Oliver Lodge. After a time John Lane ceased to produce the *Review* and Jennie gave her new name, Mrs. George Cornwallis West, as the publisher—at forty-five she had married a young officer only two weeks older than her son Winston. But the *Review* was allowed to die after the tenth issue as Jennie turned her energies towards promoting the careers of her husband and son, while Pearl returned to fiction and to preparing a series of public lectures to be given in America.

In February 1905 she wrote to a friend, confiding her concern over her pulse: 'I don't believe I shall live much longer . . . . For many years I have been trying to cheat exhaustion; my mind is as active as ever but I can't struggle against this fatigue. My life has been sad and eventful. I have lived two lives in one: I take everything to heart and I have thought far too much . . . . My knowledge of the world has not embittered me, but it has *tired* me.'

Despite melancholy forebodings she left for a long lecture tour of America in November 1905; before sailing she added £5,000 to her insurance policy, making it a total of £18,000 to be paid to her son. The tour was a great success; in each town the arrival of 'John Oliver Hobbes,' elegantly gowned, was an occasion. The lectures such as 'Balzac, Turner and Brahms,' or 'Dante and Botticelli,' juxtaposed names which seemed absurd to Max Beerbohm who imagined her delivering a lecture on 'Isaiah, Watteau and Strauss.'

She was entertained and feted by famous people of the time; when she gave a lecture at Barnard College in New York she was introduced by the former American ambassador to England; in Washington she was the guest of Mary Curzon's parents at their Dupont Circle mansion, and was invited to the White House by Theodore Roosevelt. By the end of January 1906 she was too exhausted to continue with the tour. She wrote to her clerical friend William Brown: 'I could not live in this country. It is marvelous, stimulating, all kinds of things, but it is very crude.'

In March she wrote to another friend: 'I thought I was dying last Saturday and I am sorry I did not . . . . Please don't think I want a long illness and horrors. I want to die in harness and at work . . . .' Her last months were not happy. Her former husband had re-married and was living in the Bayswater area so that she was apt to see him in the street or at the post office. She wrote about him to William Brown: 'He is an evil wretch.' She was also having trouble with George Moore, and to William Brown she wrote: 'I had an extraordinary scene with George Moore at Unwin's. He had been lying abominably abt a contract & trying to make a quarrel between Unwin & me. Hopeless of course; still he *tried* to do so. I produced a document wh. fairly paralyzed him: he apologized and crawled away. I think him half-mad . . . .'

In July 1906 Mary Curzon died and Pearl's parents reminded her that Lord Curzon was available as a possible husband, but she wrote to William Brown, ' . . . there is nothing *now* in marriage which calls to me. If I had an illusion or so, it might be different.'

The end came swiftly. After a stay with her parents at Steephill Castle on the Isle of Wight Pearl returned to London on Sunday, August 13, planning to start on a motoring holiday in Scotland with her son. On the Monday morning she was found dead in her bed, clasping a rosary. Despite opposition by her father an inquest was held, ascribing her death to cardiac failure—probably an interatrial septal defect which would permit her to reach adulthood despite recurring periods of exhaustion, but would eventually cause right-sided heart failure. Piles of letters and telegrams were received by the family; Queen Victoria and the Princess of Wales both wired their condolences; over a hundred and fifty notices of her death appeared in the British press. Many notable people attended the interment at St. Mary's Cemetery, Kensal Green, and the Requiem Mass at the Jesuit Church in Farm Street; Lord Curzon sent a magnificent wreath of orchids.

In 1908 Lord Curzon unveiled a Memorial Plaque to Pearl Craigie at The University of London. Names on the Memorial Committee included Winston Churchill, Jennie Cornwallis-West, Ellen Terry, Max Beerbohm and Edmund Gosse; while J.M. Barrie and Thomas Hardy, together with numerous duchesses and marchionesses, were among the subscribers to the Memorial Fund. Lord Curzon spoke of her 'wit and humour' and her 'brilliant conversation, sparkling as the sunlight on a stream.'

The first edition of this book consists of 650 copies designed by Ellis H. Neel Jr. and printed by KNA Press Inc. of Kennett Square, Pennsylvania. Seven copies, numbered 1-7, have been specially bound in three-quarter French morocco by the James MacDonald Co. of East Norwalk, Connecticut and have been signed by the author, designer, and publisher.

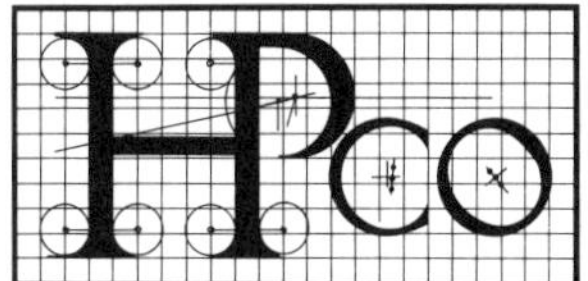